Contemporary Marketing Management

STRATEGIES AND PRACTICES

Contemporary Marketing Management

STRATEGIES AND PRACTICES

Prof. **Faheema Idrees**
Prof. **T.M. Kuthubudeen**

KW
KNOWLEDGE WORLD

KW Publishers Pvt Ltd
New Delhi

KW

KNOWLEDGE WORLD

KW Publishers Pvt Ltd

4676/21, First Floor, Ansari Road, Daryaganj, New Delhi 110002

E mail@kwpub.in/knowledgeworld@vsnl.net T +91.11.23263498 / 43528107

www.kwpub.in

ISBN 978-93-80502-46-5

Contents

Acknowledgements

We thank our Chairman, Janab Alhaj Dr S.M. Hamid Abdul Quadir, Major Dr. M. Jailani, Dean, and Dr K.E.N. Nalla Mohamed, the Principal and Dr. K. Shyama, Director, P.G. Department of Management Studies of our organisation, for giving a podium to culture the talents and shaping those amorphous thoughts to distinguishable work. Each of our family members... spouse, children and parents do have an aiding hand on this work. We thank our friends for their valuable suggestions.

We are grateful to Mr. V. Ravi and our publisher for bringing our script into the arena.

CHAPTER 1

Guerilla, Viral and Buzz Marketing

It's easy to come up with new ideas; the hard part is letting go of what worked for you two years ago, but will soon be out of date.

— Roger von Oech

Guerilla Marketing

Let's start with guerilla marketing. The term was coined and defined by Jay Conrad Levinson in his 1984 book *Guerilla Marketing*. The term has since then become a popular one for innovative marketing methods. Guerilla marketing is an unconventional method of marketing by implementing any new system of promotion that relies on time, energy and imagination rather than a big marketing budget. Typically, like guerilla warfare, the marketing tactics are unexpected and unconventional, with innovative techniques, and the consumers are targeted in unexpected and unusual places.

Guerilla marketing involves unusual and unexpected approaches. Earlier, barge-in encounters in public places, street giveaways of products and gifts, popularity, image building and personal relations were considered unconventional, but in the course of time, they have become popular and conventional methods in current usage. What is innovative at one point of time becomes stale with the passage of time. This makes the marketing people look for innovations, hatching up new ideas every now and then. Hence, any new unconventional marketing method intended to get maximum results from minimal resources is termed guerilla marketing. More innovative approaches to guerilla marketing are now utilising cutting edge mobile digital technologies and online technologies to create a buzz among the customers and synergise the buzz into reality.

Street teams are the cornerstone of guerilla success. Some brands are using event-marketing dollars to fund semi-permanent and permanent street teams in local markets. Guerilla marketing includes any activity that uses means other than the traditional media to communicate your bank's name and positioning to your prospects. Also called "extreme marketing," "grassroots marketing," or even "feet-on-the-street marketing," a guerilla campaign has no preset rules or boundaries. As such, guerilla marketing can work for businesses of all sizes. If executed properly, a guerilla campaign can be a low-cost, high-impact way to connect with business prospects.

Levinson[1] identifies the following principles as the foundation of guerilla marketing:

- Guerilla marketing is specifically geared for small businesses and entrepreneurs.
- It should be based on human psychology instead of experience, judgment, and guesswork.
- Instead of money, the primary investments of marketing should be time, energy, and imagination.
- The primary statistic to measure business is the amount of profits, not sales.
- The marketer should also concentrate on how many new relationships are made each month.
- Create a standard of excellence with an acute focus instead of trying

---

1. Jay Conrad Levinson, *The Guerilla Marketing Handbook* (Houghton Mifflin, 1984).

to diversify by offering too many diverse products and services.

- Instead of concentrating on getting new customers, aim for more referrals, more transactions with existing customers, and larger transactions.
- Forget about the competition and concentrate more on cooperating with other businesses.
- Guerilla marketers should always use a combination of marketing methods for a campaign.
- Use current technology as a tool to empower your business.

Guerilla Street Marketing

As a part of guerilla street marketing, people are dressed up like cartoon characters to promote the products they sell. Many big companies use such advertising, especially to make children happy. For instance, Mc Donald, one of the successful fast food retailers, exhibits live cartoon characters to make the kids happy.

Source: www.cherryflava.com/.a/6a00d83451aee269e20120..

Case 1: Lessons in Customer Service from Wal-Mart

The customers were regarded and treated as guests at Wal-Mart. The company was known for its warm reception, with the staff greeting the customers with a warm welcome and a friendly smile, the moment they entered a store. When the customers entered the mall, men at service offered the customers shopping carts and conveyed to them that Wal-Mart was glad to have them at the store. Regular customers at Wal-Mart were made to feel important by being addressed by their names.

Customers were looked after completely by providing full attention to their needs. If customers asked where a product could be found, they were not merely shown the way, but were actually accompanied to the correct location. Even customers making low-value transactions were treated with the same respect and courtesy. All customers were allowed to exchange products or seek refunds for products if they wished.

An important practice at Wal-Mart that could work for the benefit of customers was the "Sundown rule". According to the Sundown rule, the staff had to resolve all service-related requests made by customers before the sun set. The rule aimed to induce a sense of urgency in meeting customer service requests. The quick response to customer calls demonstrated Wal-Mart's dedication to better customer service. In most cases, the customers' problems were dealt with immediately. In case they were not put right the same day, the staff kept the customers informed about the action being taken.

Wal-Mart's pricing policies always aimed at recognising that consumers want the best bargain on the products purchased by them, without compromising on the quality. Walton had used the captions "We Sell for Less" and "Satisfaction Guaranteed" on the very first Wal-Mart signboard. Wal-Mart followed what it called the Every Day Low Price (EDLP) policy.

Attractions for Guerilla Marketing

- Guerilla marketing gives personal attention to the customer.
- It comes as a surprise and, hence, gives happiness to the customer.
- As it is an unconventional method, it is much talked about.

- The public will pay attention to this kind of promotion.
- The product is remembered long after, for many years.

Guerilla Advertising

Water is the best therapy to keep the skin wrinkle free.

Source: http://in.yahoo.co./s/136031/t_3_story_1

Agency: Crush Art Director: David Seah Copy Writer: Terence Leong

Source: http://creativecriminal.blogspot.com/2006/05/this-is-interesting-piece-of-guerilla.html

This is an advertisement for transparent images that can be pasted on cars. This guarantees that people will take a look at the car.

Agency: Mudra DDB, Chennai, India Client: Natural Hair Care - Henna Powder

Source: http://2.bp.blogspot.com/_g_nCIf2c1UE/SdoO3WNEpEI/AAAAAAAAAo8/
eMOl1fTS0jE/s1600-h/Natural + Hair + Care_800.jpg)

This is an advertisement for henna. It is interesting to note that the hair is entirely designed with henna. This will attract people as it is very artistically displayed.

Wherever art mingles with science and technology, there is a high intensity of creativity and a high magnitude of attraction. This makes the advertising work better as customers take notice of the product. It helps to single out an advertisement from the many available.

Creating an advertisement is itself an art but providing the art in a surprising way makes it guerilla advertising. It is a part of communication. Hence, it should not give false information in the name of creativity. And, advertisers should remember that there is thin line of difference between creativity and stupidity. Hence, this line should not be crossed on any aspect. Even very big advertising agencies and big products have failed in this area. They should keep in mind the creativity sensing ability of their target group. The best advertisement might not be a successful one.

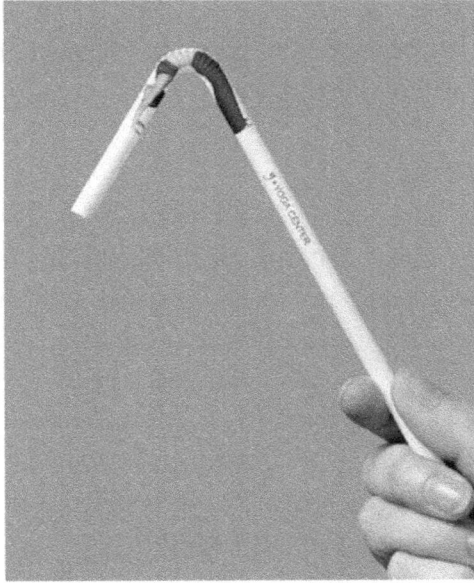

Source: funnymos.com) This is an advertisement for a yoga centre. The bend of the straw is used effectively to depict a yoga exercise.

Guerilla marketing warfare strategies are designed to wear down the customers by minor attacks, using the principle of surprise and hit-and-run tactics. Guerilla marketing was initially used by small and medium enterprises (SMEs), whereas, it is now increasingly being adopted by large businesses.

Sky Writing: Companies used to write the brand name of a product in the sky with the help of small aircraft by propelling fumes or some sprays forming the brand name in the clouds. This type of promotional technique is used where there is a large gathering witnessing some big event like sports, etc.

Marketing becomes tougher without financial resources. Hence, small enterprises managing with less resources opt for this type of marketing though the big marketers prefer to be innovative but more in Research

& Development (R&D) than in marketing. This is not a single marketing method, rather a combination of unmatching techniques combined in an unusual way that justifies the product.

Tissue Pack Marketing

The origins of this date back to the late 1960s when Hiroshi Mori, the founder of a paper-goods company in Kochi Prefecture called Meisei Industrial Co. was looking for ways to expand the demand for paper products. Japanese companies market the product by distributing tissue paper packs in public spots. This tissue pack is easy to carry, foldable, easy to use and useful for personal use. It was successful as people tend to use the tissues whereas flyers are immediately discarded. The customers responded — at least they looked at it before throwing it away. This is a cheap as well as an effective strategy.

Japan is still the main market for tissue-pack advertising, but the practice has begun to spread overseas as many Japanese companies operate worldwide. This is an effect of the global market. An innovative idea spreads like a virus throughout the world.

Pizza box advertising is one of the most effective ways to get premiere placement for your message or brand inside the consumers' homes, dorms and offices.

Forehead Advertising is an advertising concept that uses people's foreheads as advertising spaces. Forty people with Toyota Scion logos on their foreheads walked around Times Square to promote Toyota's newest Scion. Cunning of London worked with Toyota to create the campaign.

Andrew Fischer, from Omaha, Nebraska, US, is the highest bidder on Ebay for renting his forehead for advertisements, like a billboard.

Source: http://news.bbc.co.uk/2/hi/technology/4161413.stm

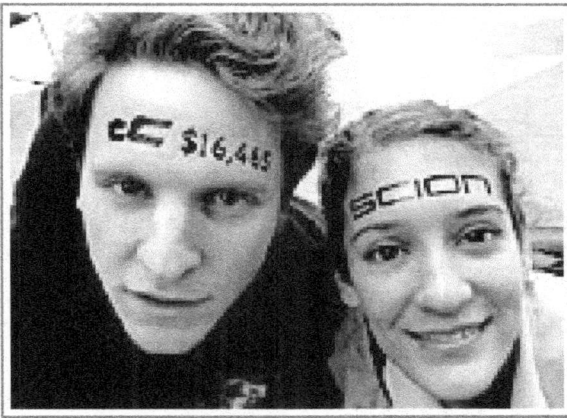

Source: http://cellar.org/iotd.php?threadid=5546) **Undertoad** Wednesday
Apr 14 01:13 PM

Body Ads

Apart from forehead advertising that is highly popular, there are body writing practices where the entire body is given on lease for an advertisement.

Animation and Claymation Advertising

Throughout the world, animation has been a successful concept. Walt Disney's success is evidence of its popularity. Many product mascots are now being created and successfully launched for various products: the Air India Maharaja, Amul girl, Pillsbury doughboy, 7 Up's Fido-dido, ICICI's Chintamani, Frito Brandito for Frito corn chips and Vodafone's Zoo Zoos. They are created not only for baby products but for various other products.

These animated characters are easily remembered in the long run. The character is often personified with certain characteristics and behavioural patterns.

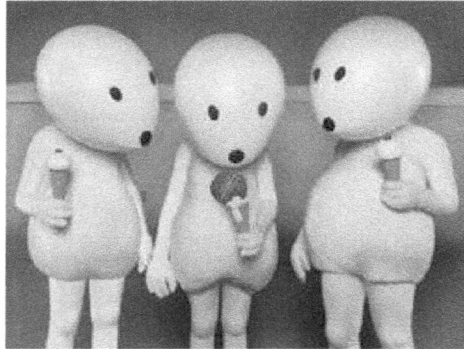

Source: http://abhisays.com/marketing/watch-vodafone-zoozoo-ads-online.html)

Offers as a Promotional Tool

Offers play a vital role in purchasing a product. What will you offer? Free samples? This works to some extent for new products. But for other, usual products, what can be offered? An extra percentage of the product? This will imply that the sample pack has been added to the original product. Instead... offer a holiday, which is totally unrelated to the product, or offer a scholarship. This will work well.

Laser Writing

As the steady growth of digital technology continues day by day, innovation of ideas with technology rules the marketing world. In a big event gathering, laser writing is often preferred. Sky writing is done over an open auditorium and can be done in a closed auditorium too.

Though guerilla marketing is undertaken as a hidden promotion measure, it does not hide the intention of the marketing. If the intention is concealed and the product is marketed, it is called undercover marketing which will be dealt with later in this book under unethical marketing.

Though there are innumerable methods that are innovative, each company has to devise its own pioneering method for a successful campaign that should appeal to the customer in some way.

Live Buzz Marketing / Buzz Marketing

There are no facts, only interpretations.

— Friedrich Nietzsche

In buzz marketing, consumers are made to talk about the product through an event or a promotional campaign. It is otherwise termed live buzz marketing. The term 'live' indicates an actual event — not a recorded one. Hence, live buzz marketing is stated as:

A marketing technique that makes use of an actual event or performance to create word of mouth
— Justin Kirby and Paul Marsden

Buzz marketing is synonymously termed as word of mouth marketing, echo marketing, and gossip marketing, though there is slight variation between word of mouth marketing and buzz marketing. Word of mouth (WOM) aims at individuals talking about the product whereas in buzz marketing, the individuals are made to talk about the product through an event. Live buzz marketing can generate large amounts of Press coverage and PR. Messages covered by the buzz programme are hard to ignore.

Word of mouth marketing is a key component of the growth of a small business. It's often word of mouth marketing that keeps small businesses running in their early days of operation when there is little or no marketing budget. The consumers share their experience with the products or services with their family and friends. This increases the consumer base as well as the sales. Buzz marketing is a viral marketing technique that attempts to make each encounter with a consumer appear to be unique, spontaneous personal exchange of information instead of calculated marketing.

Though there are many theories that promote WOM as an effective marketing tool, it has been over-hyped. But nowadays, word of mouth has gone global through the Internet.

Referral marketing is a structured and systematic process that maximises word of mouth potential. It is a pre-planned word of mouth marketing where the buzz is created intentionally. Referral marketing does this by encouraging, informing, promoting and rewarding customers and contacts to think and talk as much as possible about the supplier, company, product and service and the value and benefit the supplier brings to them and the people they know.

Referral marketing takes word of mouth from the spontaneous and immediate situations and surroundings. Online referral marketing, using digital marketing as a platform, is the Internet-based successor to traditional referral marketing.

Covert advertising is advertising a product through the media as a part of itself. For example, a movie star uses a product throughout a show. It entices the fans and the followers of the star to use the product. For example, if a popular hero of a particular movie comes in a specific brand of car, that brand gets associated with the character of the movie.

Electronic Buzz

Buzz campaigns are now being initiated in chat rooms where marketing representatives assume an identity appropriate to their target audience and pitch their products. Personal web logs (blogs) are another popular medium for electronic buzz marketing campaigns; advertisers seek out authors of the "right kind of blog" and trade products or currency for promotion. Instant messaging (IM) applications are also being looked at as a vehicle for carrying out buzz marketing campaigns with either people or IM blogs doing the pitching.

The art of generating word of mouth has grown far more sophisticated since the early days of simple publicity stunts. Marketers believe there is no use in attacking customers through advertisements. Instead, the message has to be passed on smoothly, with credible support. Rather than blitzing the airways with 30-second TV commercials for its new Focus subcompact, Ford Motor Co. (**F**) recruited just a handful of trendsetters in a few markets and gave them each a Focus to drive for six months. In a successful campaign, each carefully cultivated recipient of the brand message becomes a powerful carrier, spreading the word to yet more carriers, much as a virus rampages through a given population. Ultimately, the brand benefits because the impact of an accepted member of the social circle will always be far more credible than the impact of any other form of advertisement on the purchaser. Sometimes, the tactics can be downright dangerous — some critics of advertising are decrying buzz marketing as a form of cultural corruption at a time when advertising already pervades the landscape.

This is particularly true when it comes to younger consumers, who, because they are still forming their brand preferences, are coveted by marketers. They are more sceptical about the messages they receive. Besides, some products or services are so complex, it's hard to get the message across in a 30-second commercial.

Types of live buzz marketing.
- Live peer-to-peer marketing.
- Live performer-to-peer marketing.

Live peer-to-peer marketing uses the common man as the brand ambassador to promote and talk about a product. It is mostly unpaid and the willingness of the satisfied customer plays a major role. This can happen at any place and at any time, unintentionally. Examples: Amway and Tupperware.

Live performer-to-peer marketing uses trained and qualified performers scripted for the role of brand ambassadors. These performances may change with the performer, stage, event and audience. There are three types of performer-to-peer marketing, namely,
- Secret performer-to-peer marketing.
- Disclosed performer-to-peer marketing.
- Overt performer-to-peer marketing.

Secret Performer-to-Peer Marketing
The consumers are never aware that they are the target of focus. The performer spreads product information and creates a buzz around it.

Disclosed Live Marketing
The consumers / audience are not aware that they are being targeted for marketing while coming for the programme but become aware during the course of the programme. This is not the same as secret performer-to-peer marketing, in which the customers do not understand that they have been used as advertising agents.

Advantages
- Many reports say that a live performance is more effective than other forms of promotion.
- It is an original idea with a creative script and a talented performer. It is often a memorable show.
- A live performance has a longer recall period.

Overt Live Buzz Marketing
The target audience is informed about the ongoing marketing by the performer and they show interest in the product and the performer. These programmes combine communication and entertainment. Overt live buzz marketing is a complex mechanism which is an output of the socio-political environment. This type of marketing refers to social and

political problems. The Apartheid system in South Africa did not allow blacks to undergo formal education. And the theatrical method was followed to bring awareness among the blacks and to protest against the whites. It has a long history — every country has attempted to resolve socio-political problems through marketing them by this method.

Advantages
- The marketing advantages are made clear to the customers.
- High public relations potential.
- Highly effective.
- Generates a voluminous database.
- Creates potential buyers.
- Converts potential buyers into real customers.

Viral Marketing

> *Social media offers new opportunities to activate...brand enthusiasm.*
> — Stacy DeBroff, founder and CEO of Mom Central

The term viral marketing was coined by Tim Draper, and Jeffrey Rayport, a member of the Harvard Business School faculty later popularised it in his 1996 Fast Company article "The Virus of Marketing". Viral marketing describes any strategy that encourages individuals to pass on a marketing message to others, creating the potential for exponential growth in the message's exposure and influence.

Viral marketing is: "The promotion of a service or product by using existing customers to pass along a marketing pitch to friends, family, and colleagues."

Viral marketing is basically spreading information in faster and manifold ways like a virus. There are speedier ways of passing information in this digital world but people still believe that the most authentic and reliable way is 'word of mouth'. Hence, the term viral marketing term is often replaced by the term buzz marketing. In reality, there is a difference that needs to be dealt with by a word of caution. Word of mouth is slow and it reaches a smaller group, like in relationship marketing. Word of mouth marketing is done among the customer's near ones, whereas viral marketing is passing of information in leaps and bounds. It uses all sorts of social networks. It is fast reaching to umpteen customers. Nowaday, viral marketing has become synonymous with online marketing. Customers are everywhere, hence, the reach is all over. It uses all types of social networks.

Passion and common interest play an important role in viral marketing. This passion drives one to pass on information to others. Need and interest alone can make this possible.

There is a difference between viral marketing and online marketing. Viral marketing uses the word of mouth technique (buzz marketing) through online marketing or other social networks. That is, it uses both online and offline media. It is based on the exponential growth of marketing communication. It is all about creating a mass market for a product.

Viral marketing can use the Internet as a vehicle to reach out faster. It tends to use certain technologies. Hence, it is also termed as affiliate marketing. But it's important to also realise that the success of a viral campaign depends on the vehicles used to transmit the message. There are companies that are better virally equipped than others. In order to create a strong viral link, the message must be transported from television advertising, to radio and other extended means of broadcasting, to the power of the Internet.

Video Marketing

Many studies show that adding videos to a website increases traffic and time-on-site. Look for a major increase in online videos in 2009. If the website does not have any videos, people tend to miss such information. There should be something displayed in an interesting way for them to browse, else there are so many common sites spilled over the net that the target audience may miss it. The videos make understanding simpler and interactive video technology will make it more appealing.

Banner Ads

If a person shows interest in running banner ads on a site, but does not want to sell the ads, there are a lot of third-party ad networks that will use the available inventory (pages on your site) to run their ads, and you get a percentage of any revenue generated. This is a good option for the early period in a business when the sales staff and technology resources available are limited. This type of marketing is done by companies like Blue Lithium, Tribal Fusion and Casale Media. Banners are those hypertext linked or hot linked graphics that appear generally on the top or bottom of a webpage. As set by the Internet Advertising Bureau, the standard physical size of a banner is 468 pixels wide by 60 pixels high, and is generally limited to 15 kilobytes in memory size.

Mobile Marketing

iPhone or other similar digital mobile devices are becoming more prevalent and user-friendly these days. The number of persons accessing e-mail on a mobile device is escalating every day. Mobile marketing will finally realise its potential in the coming years, especially for local businesses such as restaurants, movie theatres and just about anyone targeting Generation Y.

Viral promotions may take the form of video clips, interactive Flash games, advergames, ebooks, branded software, images, or even text messages.

The goal of marketers interested in creating successful viral marketing programmes is to identify individuals with high Social Networking Potential (SNP) and create viral messages that appeal to this segment of the population and have a high probability of being passed along.

The classic example of viral marketing is Hotmail.com, one of the first free Web-based e-mail services.

Maruti Suzuki was an early user of digital marketing space but has used it more effectively and efficiently from 2007. Recently, the launching of the Ritz was occupying space in forums for discussion.

In the same way, the Tata Nano is more sophisticated and digital savvy, with more interacting sessions through Orkut and Facebook.

Nokia, the Finnish company, has made a remarkable milestone through creating accounts in Twitter, Orkut and Facebook. It has created Shout box for feedback.

Fanfare Sites

Organisations are more focussed on getting their customers together around other common interests. Muscledog.com is one such site. A company in the health and fitness industry worked with DP&L to create Muscledog.com, a site where potential customers interested in body-building can create profiles to share with other Muscledog.com members and interact in forums on fitness-related topics, and where this firm can post its own ads and sell ad space to others. There is intentionally no mention of the brand on the site because the company wishes to remain anonymous.

Social Media

The graph below is taken from the site Bloggation. In an article entitled "Surprising Data About the Viral Growth Through Social Media", it is clearly stated that after the entry of the social media, communication is growing in an exponential way. Growth was a little slow till the inflation

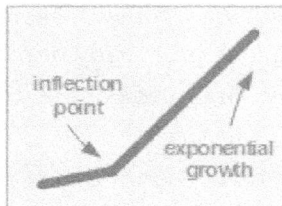

Network Effects Power the Growth of Web 2.0 Apps

inflection point

exponential growth

Caveat: The application must be designed to encourage network effects

point as the numbers of users were less. But as the total mass dwindled, it took a hockey stick graphical growth.

In a survey by Assocham (Associated Chambers of Commerce and Industry), it was found that employees spend an hour a day in social networks like Orkut, Facebook, etc. Some 84% of employees are seen as Internet addicts.

SMS-based mobile phone social networks are becoming popular now. They allow friends to mingle easily. But, in India, due to the non-availability of GPRS on all phones, its growth has been a bit slow when compared to many other countries.

Companies such as HUL, Tata Tea, Titan, and HDFC are using the peer-to-peer network on various social network sites like Orkut, Facebook or Twitter. They help their employees by providing interactive sessions through these networks. It is believed that people trust these reviews more than just a created buzz; this is also another way of creating an online buzz around the brand. Aircel has launched a voice message application on Facebook, which allows friends to leave each other voice messages instead of plain text messages.

Social Network Media Optimisation
- Foruming or forum marketing is utilising the online forum for promoting the product.
- Blogging or posting interactive blogs enables product information to be spread.

Advantages
- It is more advantageous than search engine optimisation as it reaches the target person easily.
- It focusses on individuals.
- It is easy to create more traffic.

Online Friends Network
Orkut: This the widely used social network. It was created by former

Google engineer Orkut Buyukkokten. As it is endowed with free viewing and an open nature, it led to various acquisitions like hate messages and free sex information browsing even among minors. But it has now cleaned its network and has certain security guards over such acquisitions.

Facebook: This is the world's largest social network with 200 million users. It began as small group network among Harvard students, started up by Mark Zuckerberg.

My Space: This was begun by Rupert Murdoch's News Corp and gained popularity in a big way, especially among musicians and actors.

Fropper: This is about meeting people, making new friends and having fun with photos, videos, games and blogs! Come, become a part of the strong Fropper community that is made up of four million people. All these friendship networks have certain things in common like cinema, comedy, entertainment, film and animation, health and fitness, music, news and politics, sports and travel and events.

Indiaza.com is an Indian social networking and friendship website that allows people to communicate with their Indian friends and exchange information.

Online Video Sharing

You Tube
It is gaining popularity as it allows uploading of videos — it is estimated that it is viewed every minute.

Other video sharing services are *Hulu, Vimeo* and *Daily motion.*

Online Professional Networks
LinkedIn: This is extremely popular among Indian Incorp. Most of them are premium members and have their advertisements in it. *CIO.in* is another corporate social medium.

Biznik: This is only for entrepreneurs and not for job seekers.

CEO World: A top level management network. It gives information on small business start-ups.

Cofoundr – A private social network for those seeking partners or teams for business.

Efactor – For those seeking international business collaborations.

Entreprenuer Connect – A platform to market the business, to find a potential partner, etc.

Fundfinder – Links entrepreneurs with angel investors.

The Funded — It facilitates the meet up of entrepreneurs and financiers.

First Pitch – It facilitates real-time interaction among businessmen.

Blogging

Blogging is the oldest form of read-write online social media. Anyone can create their own blog and address their opinion on any topic. Some of the free blogging services available on the Internet are Blogger/ Blog spot, Word Press and Live Journal.

MicroBlogging

Twitter is the most popular microblogging service. It is a fact that 10% of its users display 90% of its content. It is very popular whenever there is breaking news like 26/11, Michael Jackson's death, etc. As the traffic is high, there is a larger number of bluffs. It is risky to use popular microblogging services like Twitter for marketing.

Other Types of Social Networks

Social Book Marking: *Digg, Redditand Del.cio.us:* Through these social book marking spaces, any interesting, worthy and remarkable page of a book can be kept for others to view, read and enjoy.

Photo Sharing: *flickr* owned by Yahoo, *Picasa* owned by Google and *snapfish* owned by HP aids for easy photo sharing.

Music Sharing: *last fm is* for sharing and enjoying music.

Indian media sites: Big Adda, Yaari.

Many young professionals who are self-employed reach out to a large number of clients through these social media. A young tattoo professional gets lots of clients through Facebook or Twitter.

Advantages of Viral Marketing

- Large data base creation.
- Customer relationship management is effectively followed.
- Higher reach than the targeted level.
- Cost-effective.
- Creating interest, curiousity, amazement and admiration by creating a buzz around the product.
- The accountability is high when measuring its Return On Interest (ROI).
- It integrates well with the traditional marketing methods.
- The contents of viral advertising will help in spreading information. The more interesting and innovative advertisement will be disseminated faster to a larger group.

Disadvantages of Viral Marketing

- Many customers consider it as undercover marketing and, hence, illegal. This is because there is a thin line of difference between the two.
- Rebuilding the image after viral marketing is difficult. Hence, the company should be clear about its communications.

Apart from these methods, there are influential marketing and evangelist marketing. In influential marketing, the most influential person among the users is made the brand ambassador, whereas in evangelist marketing, the most loyal customer is made the brand ambassador. There are other names for viral marketing such as grassroots marketing, avalanche marketing, buzz marketing , cascading style marketing, centrifugal marketing, exponential marketing, fission marketing, organic marketing, propagation marketing, referral marketing, ripple marketing, self-perpetuation marketing, self-propagation marketing and stir marketing. These terms have the same meaning, with marginal differences.

CHAPTER 2

Online Marketing

There are managers so preoccupied with their e-mail messages that
they never look up from their screens to see what's happening in the
nondigital world.

– Mihaly Csikszentmihalyi
– Management
Internet Technology

Online Marketing

Internet marketing is defined by Dave Cheffey[1] as "achieving marketing
objectives through digital technologies."

The 21st century organisation is a learning organisation. It is highly
networked and information flows from all parts of the world. The Internet
has become a global marketplace where business organisations sell and
buy without meeting the customer. There are virtual organisations with
a minimum number of employees say, five or six, and corporations run
successfully, with a few activities contracted out. And e-shops and e-tailing
have become common buzz words of today.

---

1. Dave Cheffey, *Internet Marketing*, 3rd edition, 2006.

Apart from private organisations, electronic governance is becoming predominant in the government sector too.

CommerceNet is a consortium of companies promoting the use of the Internet for electronic commerce. The objective of this net is to help companies in business activities such as procurement and selling through transactions made easy by the net.

Advantages of the Internet.

- No ownership by anybody. The individual getting into the net is responsible for his computer and activities thereon.
- No membership fees.
- No censorship.
- No government control.
- Highly connective and heavily informative.
- Creating a global office

Internet marketing, also referred to as i-marketing, web marketing, online marketing, or eMarketing, is the marketing of products or services over the Internet.

As the marketers found that people were getting addicted to the Internet day by day in increasing numbers, they also found that they tend to avoid anything that looks like an advertisement. They shut down if advertising blogs or pop-ups come their way while they are online, though they may be in need of that information. They consider these advertisements as irritating and disturbing. Hence, the marketers wanted to trap the growing number of Internet users without disturbing them. This led to the development of social networks. Traditional media like television, radio, newspaper, hoardings in today's highly competitive world have proved to be insufficient in fulfilling the advertisers' need, as the growing population has to be reached effectively, mounting competition has to be challenged, and emerging technology has to be overtaken. So one of the solutions for this problem can be Internet advertising. Internet advertising is a communication medium with sophisticated features such as feedback and interaction in real-time.

Online marketing is highly influenced by technological advancements in the telecommunications industry. Apart from SMS, the advent of MMS has made online marketing more capable of targeting the individual. This has resulted in online branding campaigns which seek to shape consumer attitudes and feelings towards specific products. This paradigm shift has been made possible by the growth of broadband. India has a wide network which has great possibilities for the future.

How Does Internet Advertising Work?

There are various Internet advertising techniques:

1. The ad owner pays a fixed amount for each person who visits the page with the ad.
2. The ad owner pays a fixed amount for each click on an ad that links to the advertiser's website.
3. The ad owner pays a fixed rate to have his advertisement posted for a specified duration.
4. The ad owner has the option of promoting his product or service through survey-based contests on the site.

The emergence of the Internet and new information technology has led many companies to reconsider the communication process and marketing scope in a wider context than before. Early entrants and the creative marketing solution providers hold the key to success. It is a medium of growth and scope. The number of surfers will increase — more than in any other media. Porter states that some companies have used Internet technology to shift the basis of competition away from quality, features and service toward price, making it harder for anyone in their industry to reach profitability. Porter has pointed out how the Internet influences the industry structure. Some of his findings are:

• Differences among competitors are reduced.
• Competition migrates to price.
• Geographic market widens, increasing the number of competitors.

- New substitution threats are created by the proliferation of the Internet.
- Standardisation of products reduces differentiation.
- Reduced barriers to entry shifts power to suppliers.
- Traditional powerful channels are eliminated.
- The end-users' bargaining power is increased through reduced switching costs.
- It is difficult to keep Internet applications from new entrants.
- The Internet can expand the market by making the industry more efficient.

According to many people, online advertising has a dual face — legitimate and illegitimate. Legitimate online advertising involves search engine advertising, advertising networks and opt-in e-mail, whereas illegitimate online advertisement is done through spamming, search engine spamming and mousetrapping. The basic unit of Internet advertising is the banner ad which is a simple strip along the top of the webpage.

One popular type of Internet advertising strategy is article marketing campaigns through the use of search engine optimisation. This works by displaying various articles that target keywords that are directly related to a particular product. In return, the targeted traffic is driven through the website by way of hyperlinks, backlinks, and author resource boxes. Another popular type of Internet advertising is the use of social bookmarking and social networking websites. Examples include Pay per Click, Banners, Popups, Online Business Directories, etc.

Advantages of Online Marketing
- The Internet has brought many unique benefits to marketing, one being the lower costs and greater reach and distribution of information to a worldwide audience.
- It has the advantage of measuring statistics easily and inexpensively.

- Internet marketing is relatively inexpensive when compared to the ratio of cost against the reach of the target audience
- The interactive nature of Internet marketing, in terms of both providing instant response and eliciting response, is a unique quality of the medium.
- Internet marketing is sometimes considered to have a broader scope because it not only refers to digital media such as the Internet, e-mail, and wireless media, but also includes management of digital customer data and Electronic Customer Relationship Management (ECRM) systems. Internet marketing ties together creative and technical aspects of the Internet, including design, development, advertising, and sale.
- For attaining the highest rate of traffic to your website.
- For gaining an advantage over your competitors.
- To be perceived as a market leader.
- For gaining global acceptance.
- The marketer can keep track of the statistics of clicks on an advertisement, visiting a website, and performing a targeted action. Such sophistication and accuracy cannot be achieved through billboard advertising or any other form of advertising.
- Internet marketing can offer a greater sense of accountability for advertisers.
- As more and more people opt for Internet banking, they will get accustomed to Internet shopping in the near future.

Restrictions
- Computer literacy of customers.
- Low speed Internet connections.
- If the advertising is promoted through large and complicated websites, then dial-up connections or mobile devices may experience significant delays in content delivery.
- The belief of the customer in experiential buying rather than virtual shopping. Customers prefer contact with the product, especially the

tangible product, by seeing, touching and experiencing the aesthetic satisfaction before purchasing.

- Companies which can deliver value to global customers alone can have such strong conviction in this type of marketing. They should have strong logistics and channels of distribution to global customers.
- Security concerns are questionable.
- Existence of fake online companies.
- Increasing cyber thefts.
- Trick banner — a banner advertisement that attempts to trick people into clicking, often by imitating an operating system message.

Business Models

Internet marketing is associated with several business models:

- E-commerce — goods are sold directly to consumers (B2C) or businesses (B2B).
- Publishing — the sale of advertising, discussion through blogs.
- Lead-based websites — an organisation generates value by acquiring sales leads from its website.
- Affiliate marketing — a process in which a product or service developed by one person is sold by another active seller for a share of profits. The owner of the product normally provides some marketing material like sales letter, affiliate link, tracking facility. For example, the provider of the website is an affiliate marketer.

There are many other business models based on the specific needs of each person or business that launches an Internet marketing campaign.

E-mail: It was the pioneering advertisement method in online marketing but it is still effectively utilised as a medium of communication. When compared to other methods like blogs, banner ads or other forms of digital advertisement, e-mail proved itself able to reach persons personally and deliver the message. Other methods like billboards, banners or pop-ups are non-personal and common to all type of advertisements. It is, however, getting more difficult to use these as more government restrictions are being placed on them. E-mail is fast, inexpensive, easy to filter and reliable.

Newsletters: This is an extension of e-mail but is a very effective tool. If you include enough timely and valuable information, a good newsletter can drive up the number of visits to your website.

Banner Advertising

Web Banner or Banner Ad

This is another way of interacting with customers through ads. A graphic image, in the shape of a banner, advertises a site on another site. A viewer can click on the ad to view that site instantly. It is a form of advertising on the World Wide Web. The ad pictures can contain one or more hyperlinks to the products or services or to third party advertising to generate additional revenue. This form of online advertising entails embedding an advertisement into a web page. It can act as a rotating billboard ad. It is intended to attract traffic to a website by linking to the website of the advertiser. The advertisement is constructed from an image (GIF, JPEG, PNG), JavaScript programme or multimedia object employing technologies such as Silverlight, Java, Shockwave or Flash, often employing animation, sound, or video to maximise presence. Images are usually in a high-aspect ratio shape (i.e. either wide and short, or tall and narrow), hence, the reference to banners. These images are usually placed on web pages that have interesting content such as a newspaper article or an opinion piece. Image swapping or replacing of images is possible by highlighting an element. The image can be swapped by clicking the highlighted element.

Source: http://upload.wikimedia.org/wikipedia/commonos/b/bQ/Qxz-ad39.png)

There are two types of banner ads:

- Front page banners.
- Bcentral banners.

The front page banner ads display a sequence of advertisements in an organised way. The size of the banner ads can be chosen, along with the sequence of display, its duration and its transition effect .

Bcentral banner ads are cooperative networks that allow the crediting of the earning of displaying an advertisement for every two banner ads. That is, for every two banner advertisements displayed, one banner advertisement is allowed to be displayed free of cost.

Digital Billboards

There are differences between digital and regular/static billboards:

- With regard to digital billboards, ad space is shared with other advertisers. With traditional billboards, the advertiser on the billboard is the only display for the entire duration of the display period — usually a minimum of a month.
- Digital billboard advertising is new, in demand and in prime locations — it is not a recipe for bargains. Though the ad space is shared by many, the price is not less than static billboards.
- Digital billboards display the advertisements on the face of the browser so that the user cannot avoid viewing them.
- Lower production costs. Because they are digital, there is no printing, or installation to be done. Once the creativity is finished, it is simply e-mailed for display across the network or to the specific location (s).
- Instead of being tied to a single display, digital allows you to show your ad (or changing ads!) across multiple locations and without the production costs. Digital billboard networks can provide you with excellent placement at multiple locations in a market's high-traffic areas.
- Digital displays are illuminated from behind the image, making them

easy to notice — especially at night. Most billboard displays are front lit (lit from above or below the image).

Porsche launched the new Panamera through billboard advertisements.

Search Engine

A search engine is a site that indexes according to the content.

There are web search engines, selection-based search engines, metasearch engines, desktop search tools, and web portals and vertical market websites that have a search facility for online databases.

Affiliate sites are those sites that send visitors to another commercial site, usually in a related business area, in exchange for a commission, if the sale is made from the visitor who came through the affiliate site.

Source: webguild.org

The ad above is for an Ebay affiliate link. The Ebay data feeds are displayed as affiliate links, which pays for each visitor who follows the link and goes on to make a purchase on Ebay. The amount paid is 50% of the Ebay commission for the item purchased.

It is ideal to place a product on a search engine, as customers often look out for information through search engines only.

General

- Ask.com (formerly Ask Jeeves)
- Bing (formerly MSN Search and Live Search)
- Duck Duck Go
- Google
- Yahoo! Search

Accountancy

- IFACnet

Business

- Business.com
- GlobalSpec
- Nexis (Lexis Nexis)
- Thomasnet (United States)

Enterprise

- AskMeNow: S3 - Semantic Search Solution
- Concept Searching Limited: concept search products
- Dieselpoint: Search & Navigation
- dtSearch: dtSearch Engine(SDK), dtSearch Web
- Endeca: Information Access Platform
- Exalead: exalead one:enterprise
- Expert System S.p.A.: Cogito
- Fast Search & Transfer: Enterprise Search Platform (ESP), RetrievalWare Funnel back: Funnelback Search
- ISYS Search Software: ISYS:web, ISYS:sdk
- Microsoft: SharePoint Search Services
- Northern Light
- Open Text: Hummingbird Search Server, Livelink Search
- Oracle Corporation: Secure Enterprise Search 10g
- SAP: TREX
- X1 Technologies : X1 Enterprise Search
- ZyLAB Technologies: ZyIMAGE Information Access Platform

Mobile/Handheld

- Taptu: taptu mobile/social search *Job*
- Bixee.com (India)
- CareerBuilder.com (USA)
- Craiglist (by city)
- Dice.com (Technology Professionals)
- Eluta.ca (Canada)

- Hotjobs.com (USA)
- Incruit (Korea)
- Indeed.com (USA)
- LinkUp.com (USA)
- Monster.com (USA),(India)
- Recruit.net (International)
- SimplyHired.com (USA)
- Naukri.com (India)

News
- Google News
- Daylife
- MagPortal
- Newslookup
- Nexis (Lexis Nexis)
- Topix.net
- Yahoo! News

People
- Peek You
- Explode.us
- InfoSpace
- Spock
- Spokeo
- • Wink
- Zabasearch.com
- ZoomInfo

Video Games
- GenieKnows

Forum

- Omiligi

Multimedia

- Bing Videos
- blinkx
- Find Sounds
- Google Video
- Picsearch
- Podscope
- Seeqpod
- Veveo
- YouTube
- Pixsta
- Munax PlayAudioVideo
- Yahoo! Video
- TinEye

Price

- Google Product Search (formerly Froogle)
- Kekloo
- MSN Shopping
- MySimon
- PriceGrabber
- PriceRunner
- Shopping.com
- Shop Wiki
- Shopzilla
- TheFind.com

Questions and Answers
Human Answers

- Answers.com

- eHow
- Uclue
- Yahoo! Answers
- Stack Overflow
- DeeperWeb

Automatic Answers
- AskMeNow
- Brain Boost
- True Knowledge
- Wolfram Alpha

Wolfram Alpha's knowledge engine which was developed by Stephen Wolfram, has brought computational ability. It is more an answer engine than a search engine. It answers all factual queries but it may not answer in a textual method.

Blogs

Blogger or blog spot is a blog publishing system. A blog, which is an abbreviation of weblogs, is a compilation of thoughts, ideas, facts, news or anything that is on online. The term 'blog' was coined in 1999. Blogs are usually structured and organised by category and often updated every day. Pyra labs created it first but later it was taken over by Google. Picassa is an official photo sharing way which is integrated with Google now. There are

The Official **Google** Blog   Insights from Googlers into our products, technology, and the Google culture.

many bloggers available for service. We can create our own blogger through blogger.com, blogspot.com, socioGo.com, startcounter,com, Amatomu, Bloglines, BlogScope, IceRocket, Sphere & Technorati, etc.

When terrorists attacked the Taj Hotel in Mumbai, due to cost cutting activities, there were no foreign channels reporting on it except CNN, though people were news hungry. This paved the way for mobile phone reporting and reporting through more information on interactive blogs.

Advantages of Blogs
- No rules and restrictions.
- Connecting to many and passing information easily.
- Easy to start and maintain.
- Highly interactive.
- Freedom of expression.
- No need for spam filters as no e-mail is accepted since contents are written directly on the blog space.
- They have a track back system that allows visitors to know the original contributor to the blog.
- No restrictions on the number of blogs that can be created.
- They are economical.
- They are educational.
- They are search engine friendly.

Corporate Blogs
These are publications on the web working as individual microsites. They reflect thoughts, interest, opinions and information on various subjects of business. They are published with the support of organisations,

Types of Corporate or Organisational Blogs
External Blogs:

Sales blogs – They helps in promoting and selling of the product.

Relationship blogs – To strengthen the relationship with the customer and creating new customers through the existing customer base.

Branding blogs – To strengthen brand profile, building brand image and value creation.

Internal blogs – These can be viewed within the corporate organisation by the employees.

Knowledge blogs – To give employees information and insights on work, assignments, new projects, news, reports, and business information.

Collaboration blogs – To provide the team or working group with a tool for research, collaboration and discussion.

Culture blogs – To strengthen organisational culture.

Forums - Groups of people constitute forums, whereas blogs are constituted by many individuals. Forums reflect the opinion, sentiment and reaction of a group forming an online community. The outsider who visits the forum is unable to distinguish any individual – it could be a forum by college students. The contribution is named by the group.

Tags, or folksonomies are user defined methods for organising data. Some examples of tagging in operation are:

- del.icio.us - a social bookmarking system
- Flickr - a photo publishing / sharing site
- Technorati Tags - a recent feature added to the popular blog search engine
- MetaFilter Tags - another recently added feature to the original group blog.
- TagSurf - an experimental forum based on tags rather than the standard way of organising topics.

del.icio.us and flickr were the first systems to use tagging , at least to become popular because of it. They allow users to submit data, links with descriptions and photos respectively, and classify that data themselves.

You Tube
YouTube was founded by Chad Hurley, Steve Chen and Jawed Karim, who were all early employees of PayPal. As they faced some difficulty while

sharing videos of their party, they ended up creating YouTube. It is the largest video sharing website. It was later purchased by Google Inc. Unregistered members are allowed to watch while registered members can upload it.

Source: http://tech2.com/media/images/2007/may/img_6710_apple_youtube.jpg)

Different Approaches to Online

(a) One-to-One Approach

The targeted users typically browse the Internet alone, so the marketing messages can reach them personally. This approach is used in search marketing, where the advertisements are based on search engine keywords entered by the user. It is more likely that customers tend to open the first page information from Google or any other search engine rather than the last page. Hence, it is wise to advertise in the foremost place through search engines.

(b) Appeal to Specific Interests

Internet marketing places emphasis on marketing that attracts a specific behaviour or interest, rather than reaching out to all categories of people. Marketers typically segment their markets according to socio-demographic factors like age group, gender, geography, income and other general factors. Apart from this, there is the common interest group whose influence is far reaching as they are volunteers and seekers, not ignorant or uninterested individuals. Marketers have the luxury of targeting by activity and geolocation. For example, a kayak company can post advertisements on kayaking and canoeing or bungee jumping websites with the full knowledge that it will appeal to the adventurous, sport loving audience.

(c) Geotargeting

Geotargeting and geomarketing are the methods of determining the geolocation (the physical location) of a website visitor with geolocation software, and delivering different content to that visitor based on his or her location, such as country, region/state, city, metro code/zip code, organisation, Internet Protocol (IP) address, ISP or other criteria. This helps to understand the behaviour of the customers based on their geographic details. The potential of the product / service, based on location will help further market research.

(d) Different Content by Choice

A typical example for different content by choice in geotargeting is the FedEx website at FedEx.com where users have the choice to select their country location first and are then presented with different site or article content, depending on their selection.

(e) Automated Different Content

With automated different content in Internet marketing and geomarketing, the delivery of different content, based on the geographical location and other personal information, is automated.

Security System

Information security is important both to companies and consumers that participate in online business. Many consumers are hesitant to purchase items over the Internet because they are not sure that their personal information will remain private. Encryption is the primary method for implementing privacy policies. For example, a fake form of the Reserve Bank of India was on the net with an exact replica of the original form. Hence, the Government of India had to alert the public through online and offline advertisements.

Another major security concern that consumers have with e-commerce merchants is the prompt delivery of goods as per the configuration ordered. Online merchants have attempted to address this concern by investing in, and building, strong consumer brands (e.g., Amazon.com, eBay, Overstock. com). Hence, the business has to be more ethical and the delivery should fulfill the expectations of the buyer, else it may end up in demarketing not only for that particular brand but for all Internet marketers. This evokes a strong sense of commitment towards truthful display and delivery of goods to the customers. There are ways of check out like feedback rating systems and e-commerce bonding solutions. All of these solutions attempt to assure consumers that their transactions will be free of problems because the merchants can be trusted to provide reliable products and services. Additionally, the major online payment mechanisms (credit cards, Pay Pal, Google Checkout, etc.) have also provided back-end buyer protection systems as a grievance redressal system and immediate rectifying system.

Data Communication

Data communications comprise the exchange of data between two devices through some transmission medium such as wire cable. The effectiveness of data communication depends upon:

- The delivery of data to the correct destination.
- Accuracy of data.
- Timeliness.
- Jitter: refers to the variation in arriving time or deviation in the frequencies of audio and video that result in mismatching of sound and light.

Effects of Internet Marketing on Industries

Internet marketing is getting more industry oriented and its marketing methods have been exploited. Its impact on retail-oriented industries, including music, films, pharmaceuticals, banking, flea markets, as well as the advertising industry, and in manufacturing firms shows mounting growth. Internet marketing is now overtaking all offline marketing techniques, including radio and television marketing. The effect on the music industry is greater as many consumers have been purchasing and downloading music (e.g., MP3 files) over the Internet for several years in addition to purchasing compact discs.

The number of banks offering online banking has also increased. Online banking appeals to customers because it is more convenient than visiting the bank branches. Moreover, it is a more authentic, faster and easier way of banking. Most banks have gone in for Internet banking.

Indian Railways have Internet booking of tickets. Air tickets can also be booked via the Internet. Hence, the service facility is utilised in the government service sector also.

Internet auctions have gained popularity. Unique items or antique items are sold through the Internet. The products which were once found only in flea markets are being sold on Ebay. Ebay is often used as a price-basis for specialised and unusual items. Buyers and sellers look at the prices the displayed on the website before going to the flea markets.

The effect on the advertising industry has been tremendous. In just a few years, online advertising has grown to be worth tens of billions of dollars annually. Pricewaterhouse Coopers reported that US$16.9 billion was spent on Internet marketing in the US in 2006. Internet marketing has had a growing impact on the electoral process. President Barack Obama raised over US$1 million in a single day during his extensive Democratic candidacy campaign, largely due to online donors.

Extranet
This is defined as a collaborative Internet connection with other companies and business partners. An Extranet is a private network that uses Internet technology and the public telecommunication system to securely share a part of business information or operations with suppliers, vendors, partners, customers, or other businesses. It is an extension of the Internet which makes the latter accessible to outside companies or individuals with or without an Internet.

An Extranet requires security and privacy. These can include firewall server management, the issuance and use of digital certificates or similar means of user authentication, encryption of messages, and the use of Virtual

Private Networks (VPNs) that tunnel through the public network.

Companies can use an Extranet to:

- Exchange large volumes of data using Electronic Data Interchange (EDI)
- Share product catalogues exclusively with wholesalers or those in the trade.
- Collaborate with other companies on joint development efforts.
- Jointly develop and use training programmes with other companies.
- Provide or access services provided by one company to a group of other companies, such as an online banking application managed by one company on behalf of affiliated banks.
- Share news of common interest exclusively with partner companies.

The Interactive Advertising Bureau (IAB) has issued guidelines and regulations of Internet advertising. The IAB comprises more than 375 leading media and technology companies that are responsible for selling 86% of online advertising in the United States.

Case 1

Insead, a Global Learning Environment has gone beyond online or virtual university. Students can enroll themselves in the MBA programme at this virtual university. They have to animate themselves and the animated self will attend the classroom and subsequently undergo the entire student life. Apart from that, a parallel virtual economy is there, where people can buy or sell assets which are not really present but are virtually available. Though the assets are not real, the transaction and the money involved is real. There is the formation of an entire economy from industries to hospitals, education to entertainment.

Members can have a second life or a parallel life in a parallel world. This life too will have entirely the same kind of money exchanges like real life. This economy is growing bigger and bigger as there are many adapters entering this virtual economy.

Question.
1. Is this creation of virtual economy ethical?
2. Is it not an induced schizophrenia?

CHAPTER 3

Ambient and Experiential Marketing

There's a way to do it better—find it.

— Thomas Edison

This chapter deals with ambient marketing, its creativity and its reachability. Apart from that, it deals with visual merchandising and experiential marketing.

Ambience Marketing

The dictionary meaning of the word 'ambience' is, "Something that surrounds or invests; as, air . . . being a perpetual ambient."

In marketing terms, ambient marketing or advertising is also known as place based marketing. It is a promotion done at an unusual places in such a way that the surrounding or the environment complements the product.

To get your new business off to a solid start, combining two proven techniques — strategic partnering and place-based or "ambient," marketing — works well. It comprises using the environment to advertise. For example, 'No smoking' signs near the mirrors in toilets in cinema halls, product advertisements on the handle of shopping carts, etc.

Ambient Advertising

Ambient means about the environment. Advertising that is basically promoted at odd, unexpected and relevant places is called ambient advertisement.

The use of this term, initiated by the British media, has become a standard marketing term. It refers to almost any kind of advertising that occurs in some non-standard medium outside the home. Ambient advertising is the process of surrounding the target market with advertising material e.g. advertisements on till receipts, street furniture, taxis, petrol nozzles, etc. It needs large gatherings of people at places like supermarkets, car parks, leisure arenas. For Volvo, the in-port racing event represents a significant opportunity for ambient advertising as there are large numbers of people gathered at the port to greet the teams and view the in-port racing activity.

Other examples are messages on the reverse of car park receipts, the human ad carriers, the hanging straps in railway carriages, the handles of supermarket trolleys, the sides of egg cartons and almost the spaces that can be exploited for such use. It also includes such techniques as projecting huge images on the sides of buildings, or slogans on hot air balloons. These advertisement carriers are known as ambient media and the advertiser who is using this technique is called an ambient advertiser.

Amnesty International often comes up with very impressive campaigns. Just before the Olympics started last summer, the Non-Governmental Organisation (NGO) started a campaign against the repression of human rights in China. Protesting against the death penalty, these human rights activists created ambient advertisements on Hamburg buses. They hung paper bodies from the rings that standing passengers hold onto in buses. These evoked a striking reaction among the commuters.

Ambient advertising becomes lethal when the innovative idea fails or a creative idea becomes common or the environment does not justify the promotion of the product. The genuine impact of ambient media is difficult to measure as it often takes TV and Press coverage to attract wider public attention to it.

Ambient media is a term which was first used by the British media in 1999. It has become a common term now. It is the name given to the out of home surroundings that act as vibrant media vehicles. It is also known as non-traditional or alternative media. As the reach of ambient media is limited to an area, it always used in conjunction with mainstream traditional media. The key to a successful ambient media campaign is to choose the best media format available, combined with an effective message.

The following are some reasons for the growth of ambient media:

- A decline in the power of traditional media.
- Creativity and growth of out of home advertising.
- A greater demand for point-of-sale communications.
- Its ability to offer precise audience targeting.
- Its effectiveness and eye catching art work.
- Its general versatility.

The advertisement below (Fig 1) shows a shop shutter as an ambient vehicle.

Fig 1

Source: Eine's shoppershutter in London.jpg)

The shutters of shops are common carriers of advertisements. They are also the point of sale advertising but differ in a way, as, when the shop is open, the advertisement is not displayed. But when the shutters are down, it becomes an advertisement hoarding. Whether this is it ambient advertising or just the address/ identity of the shop is debatable.

The advertisement below (Fig 2) shows a woman carrying a bag. As the advertisement is from a fitness company, the handle of the bag has utilised by making it look like exercising equipment. The handle performs the role of an advertisement banner. This advertisement uses the ambience of the store to move outside as a mobile ad vehicle. This bag is carried on the roads and proves to be of interest to every passerby. This advertisement is commented upon — people talk about the product, its advertising creativity and so on.

In the same way, Fig 3, which is an advertisement for FedEx office stationery, uses the zebra crossing on the road to marks its FedEx whitener. It is effectively and creatively utilised to make it appear as though the white stripes on the road are due to the whitener and also it depicts its uninterrupted flow and clarity.

Fig 2

Source: http://adland.tv/ooh/strong-enough)

Fig 3

Source: www. Fedex.com

The advertisement below (Fig 4) shows the use of a manhole by a coffee company.

Fig 4

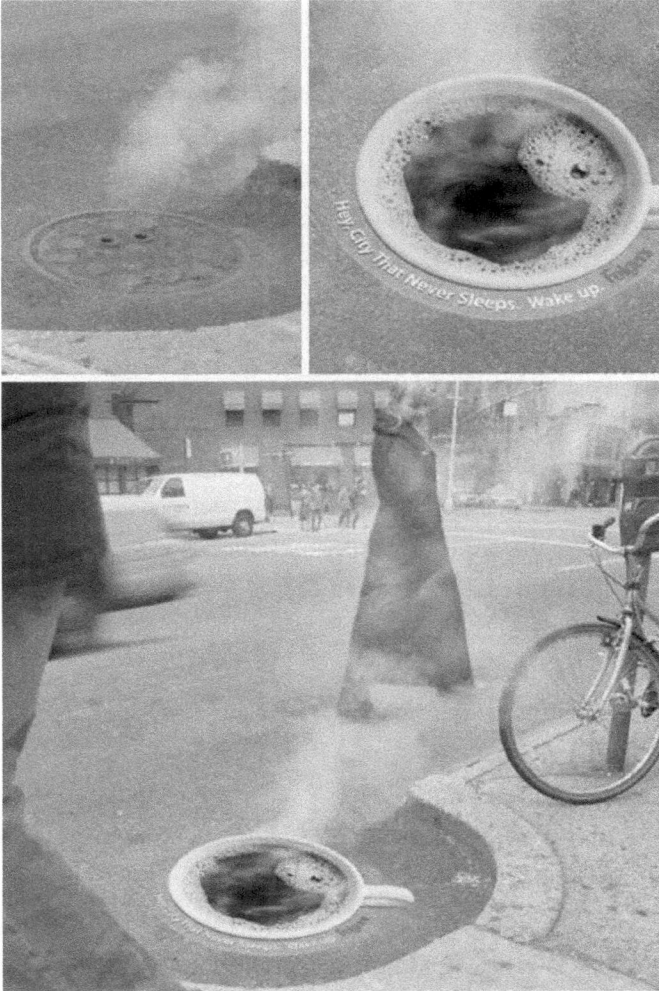

Source: posima.com/images/uploads/folgers.jpg

Experiential Marketing

Experiential marketing is a type of marketing that allows the customer to have a sense of the product, its benefit and its supremacy over other products by creating and providing a perfect environment. It should allow customers to engage with the product and provide a sense of satisfaction. It should also provide a platform for increasing revenues.

Ambient marketing emphasises the retailer's point of view whereas experiential marketing emphasises the customer's point of view. It is more about customer experience, brand experience, and retail experience.

Experiential marketers say the consumer doesn't exist anymore. In this age, we are all "prosumers," which the International Experiential Marketing Association (IXMA) describes as "the enlightened and empowered consumer... who no longer responds to a media-propelled 'brand essence.'"

Traditional marketing views consumers as rational decision-makers who care about functional features and benefits. In contrast, experiential marketers view consumers as rational and emotional human beings who are concerned with achieving pleasurable experiences.

There are five different types of experiences, or strategic experiential modules (SEMs) that marketers can create for customers:

- Sensory experiences (SENSE).
- Affective experiences (FEEL).
- Creative cognitive experiences (THINK).
- Physical experiences.
- Behaviour and lifestyle (ACT).
- Social-identity experiences that result from relating to a reference group or culture (RELATE).

"These experiences are implemented through so-called experience providers (ExPros) such as communications, visual and verbal identity, product presence, electronic media, etc. The ultimate goal of experiential marketing is to create holistic experiences that integrate individual experiences into a holistic Gestalt."[1]

---

1   Bernd Schmitt, *Handbook on Brand & Experience Management.*

An experiential approach to launch a brand may be more effective and relevant than anything that television/print advertisements can offer. For example, Mahindra wanted to launch HyTec, a strong hydraulic tractor. To show this technology to farmers, they engaged them through a technique in which sensors were fixed to the hydraulic tractor and a large LCD monitor was placed to capture the movements of the cultivator on an ECG graph. This activity was easily understood and remembered by the farmers and the sales graph increased tremendously.

Experiential marketing gives customers an opportunity to engage and interact with brands, products, and services in sensory ways that provide the icing on the cake of information providing. It is indeed experiential marketing that helps buyers make a better purchase decision. Even in the film industry, actors appear on live shows to talk about movies. "Experience providers" comprise visual identity, communication, product presence, web sites, and services to create different types of customer experiences. Today, people have become more circumspect while shopping.

Jensen identifies six types of markets based on brand experience:
- The market for adventure.
- The market for togetherness (friendship and love).
- The market for care (giving and receiving).
- The who I am market.
- The market for peace of mind.
- The market for conviction.

Brands for adventure:

Brands like trekking costumes, sports car or other requirements for mountain travellers or night riders, etc., come under this category.

Sony style store:

Sony and its co-brand Comcast showcase its latest and future products in retail shops. It has displayed "The Future of High Speed Internet" and " The Future of Home Phone Service."

The picture below (Fig 5) is of the Sony store. It facilitates customers with experiences of Sony's products. It is a highly futuristic store, mainly concerned with the provision of experiences.

Fig 5

Source: http://www.flickr.com/photos/playstationblogeurope/4197571500/

The advertisement in Fig 6 a makes the customer feel that the cars are in safe hands and will better for the treatment provided. It is focussed on those customers who pamper their cars with decorative items and worry about their working conditions unnecessarily. This clinic-like outlook provides them mental satisfaction and healing relief. There are two rooms displayed in the ad where, in the room named "Hear it", the sound system can be tested and all sound related problems can be solved. In the other room are the spares which can be purchased. This is a unique system of automotive maintenance which provides an interactive experience to the customer.

Fig 6 a

Fig 6 b

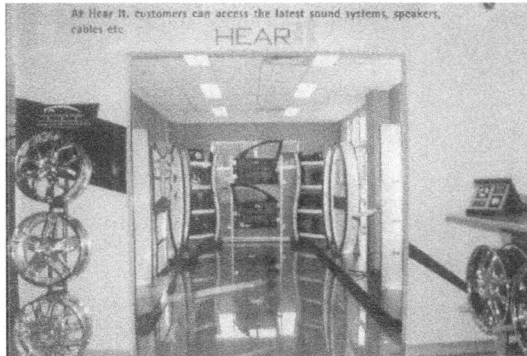

Fig 6 c

An automotive mechanic shop that is designed like a health clinic. Source: *Visual Merchandising & Retail Designing*, Jul-Aug/ Vol 4/Issue 6/ p. 28.

Experiential marketing is often obtained through visual merchandising.

Visual Merchandising

Merchandising which evolved as visual merchandising is the activity of promoting the sale of goods, especially by their presentation in retail outlets. (*New Oxford Dictionary of English*, 1999, Oxford University Press).

Visual merchandising comprises not only displaying the goods and services but is the art of creating an environment for displaying the product and service in a better way. This includes combining the product, environment, and space into a stimulating and engaging display to encourage the sale of a product or service. It has become an important element in retail. It is a team effort involving senior management, architects, merchandising managers, buyers, visual merchandising director, designers, and staff. The retailer has to design and create it in the store building itself. Many elements can be used by visual merchandisers in creating displays including colour, lighting, space, product information, sensory inputs such as smell, touch, and sound as well as technologies such as digital displays and interactive installations. The store presentation is more important and there are certain areas to be assessed like lighting, store fit-outs, colour designs, A/V quality, payment counter, wall coverings and claddings, engineered woods, product accessibility show window, flooring and service.

Visual merchandising is not a science; there are no absolute rules. It is more like an art in the sense that the usage of colours, textures, patterns, lighting, design and fashion creation make it more appealing. The main goal of visual merchandising is to improve the number of footfalls, increasing sales and exciting customers through creative displays. It helps to build the image that the company wants to project. If it does not sell, it is not visual merchandising. The look and feel of the displays determine how long the customer will spend in the shop.

Recently, visual merchandising has gained in importance as a quick and cost-effective way to revamp retail stores. There should be a sense of a place. From being a more general common outlet, it has become theme specific.

A close sister to visual merchandising is "retail experience". "Customer experience" and "brand experience" look at the same issues around product presentation but from the customer's perspective, rather than the retailer's perspective. On World Environment Day, Helios, India's largest multi-brand watch boutique, sent a go green message at Koramangala, Bangalore. It emphasised the importance of recycling by displaying a scrapture made out of watch scraps. Nearly 4,500 scrap parts were used to make a globe. The display was enhanced by a window presentation of 1,800 fluttering butterflies over potted plants.

Merits
- Attracting the customers in a creative way.
- Creating a niche for the product.
- Focussing on the target audience through creative displays.
- Educating customers in a creative way.
- Enabling long lasting impact and recall value.
- Setting the company apart in an exclusive position and maintaining brand image.
- Establishing a linkage among fashion, product design and marketing by keeping the product in prime focus.
- Combining the creative, technical and operational aspects of a product and the business.

Demerits
- Costly.
- Needs creative directors.
- Increases product cost.
- Design should be effective.
- Market segment may be narrow.

Nowadays both the customers and retail shoppers think that visual merchandising plays a major role in attracting customers. Customers like window shopping, lounge shopping and informative shopping, whereas retail shoppers need building a brand image, attention seeking, price worthy displays and high footfalls in their shops. This has paved the way in working out creative displays. Fig 7 shows how the background complements the attire on sale.

Fig 7

Source: *Visual Merchandising & Retail Designing*, Jul-Aug/ Vol 4/Issue 6/ pg. 58.)

For creating visual appeal, the designer needs to concentrate on so many things. A few are given below.

- Counters and showcases.

- Modular display fixtures.
- Slatwall and accessories.
- Slot standards.
- Shelving.
- Hangers and racks accessories.
- Jewel displayers.
- Lights and lamps.
- Sign and literature holders.
- Pricing tags.
- Bins and baskets.
- Glass display units.
  Etc...,

Fig 8

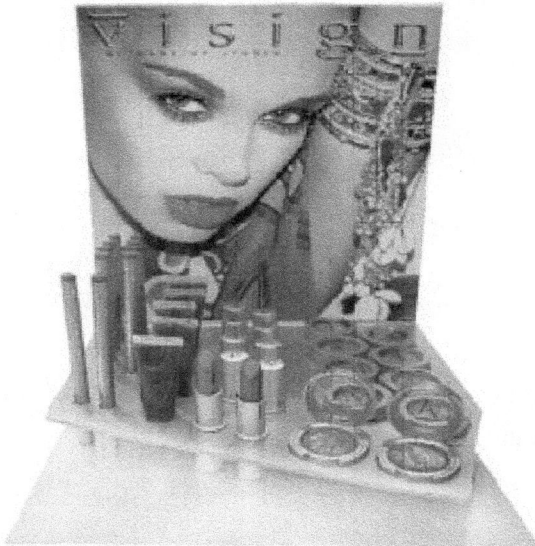

Source: http://www.beliplus.com/display-primavera-verano-2008-visign-ref_9831.html

Fig 9

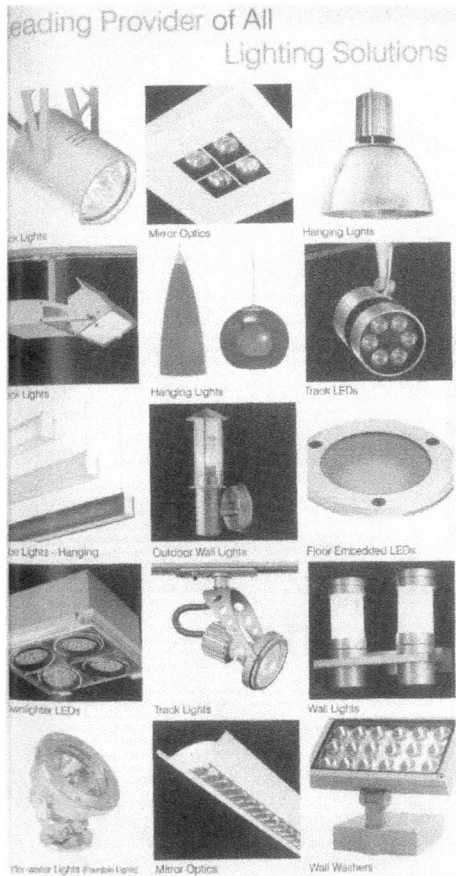

Various types of designer or decorative lights used for visual merchandising.

Source: Visual Merchandising & Retail Designing, Jul-Aug/ Vol 4/Issue 6

Experiential Marketing on Streets

Experiential marketing is an age-old concept though its growth and realisation of value is greater in the present environment. Even street-sellers who are experts in direct selling often provide the podium for experiential marketing. Road shows are based on it. They allow customers to use the product and explain how to use it, more comfortably than in a showroom environment.

Difference between ambient and experiential marketing.

- Ambient marketing need not be costly whereas experiential marketing is mostly a costly business.
- Ambient advertising uses anything in the environment effectively whereas experiential marketing uses the designed and creative things attractively.
- Ambient advertising can be targeted at the middle class whereas experiential advertising is mostly targeted at the upper class audience.

CHAPTER 4

Relationship and Permission Marketing

Quality means doing it right when no one is looking.

– Henry Ford

Relationship Marketing

Relationship marketing is, "The process of creating, maintaining, and enhancing strong value-laden relationships with customers and other stakeholders," according to Kotler and Armstrong in *Principles of Marketing*.

Berry (1983) defined it as, "It is the process of attracting, maintaining and in multi-service organizations, enhancing customer relationships."

Shani and Chalsani[1] (1992) viewed relationship marketing as "an integrated effort to identify, maintain and build up a network with individual customers and to continuously strengthen the network for the mutual benefit of both sides, through interactive, individualized and value added contracts over a long period of time."

1. David Shani and Sujana Chalasani, "Exploiting Niches Using Relationship Marketing", *Journal of Consumer Marketing*.

Wikipedia defines relationship marketing, thus, "It is that form of marketing... in which emphasis is placed on building longer term relationships with customers rather than on individual transactions."

Jim Ryan, President and CEO of Carlson Marketing Group observes, "Marketing disciplines in and of themselves are not relationship marketing.... only when orchestrated in alignment with a company's strategic objectives do they represent true relationship marketing."[2]

Relationship marketing is not about having or maintaining a virtuous and excellent relationship with your customers. Customers do not want or expect this from a marketer. Relationship marketing uses the event-driven tactics of customer retention marketing, but treats marketing as a process over time rather than as single unconnected events. Customers are induced to come for repeated purchases and for providing customer or business referrals. "Relationship" refers to the customer's purchase history.

The relationship marketing process is usually defined as a series of stages. Many different names are given to these stages, depending on the marketing perspective and the type of business. For example, working on the relationship from the beginning to the end. This type of marketing is also termed as "defensive marketing" which attempts to reduce customer turnover and increase customer loyalty. This customer-retention approach is considered defensive in contrast with "offensive marketing" which aims at obtaining new customers and liberating the old or dissatisfied customers. A successful company may be product focussed, technology focussed or infrastructure focussed but the success cannot be sustained for long if it is not customer focussed.

What is not relationship marketing?
- It is not about relationships.
- It is not about transparency.
- It is not about providing business.
- It is not about being social or using social networks.

2. Sumantha Dutta, *Relationship Marketing – A Paradigm of 21st Century*, Kolkata.

Then, what is relationship marketing?
- It is about marketing.
- It is about a customer retention strategy.

Relationships between a company and its customers, distributors, employees, and referral sources are vital for continuous, stable and sustained growth of the marketing firm. Loyal relationships with these valued individuals make for a strong bottom line. These loyal customers could be referrals for creating a second level of customers. They simply act as lead generators. Creating a retention strategy is extremely difficult as the company needs to be a solution provider even after the sale has taken place. It is answerable for every grievance of the customer about the product, its after sales service and the comparative statements of the product and service.

Table 1

Difference Between Transactional Marketing and Relationship Marketing[3]

Factors	Transactional marketing	Relationship marketing
Time	Short-term focus	Long-term focus
Price sensitivity	Customers are more sensitive to the price	Customers tends to be less sensitive to the price
Role of marketing function	Appropriate marketing mix programme	Interactive marketing
Measuring of customer satisfaction	Monitoring market share	Managing the customer
Customer related service	Little emphasis on customer related service	Strong emphasis on customer related service
Quality dimension	Quality is the sole responsibility of production	Quality is the concern for everyone

---

3. Dr. N.K. Sehgal, Gronroos,1994, 2007.

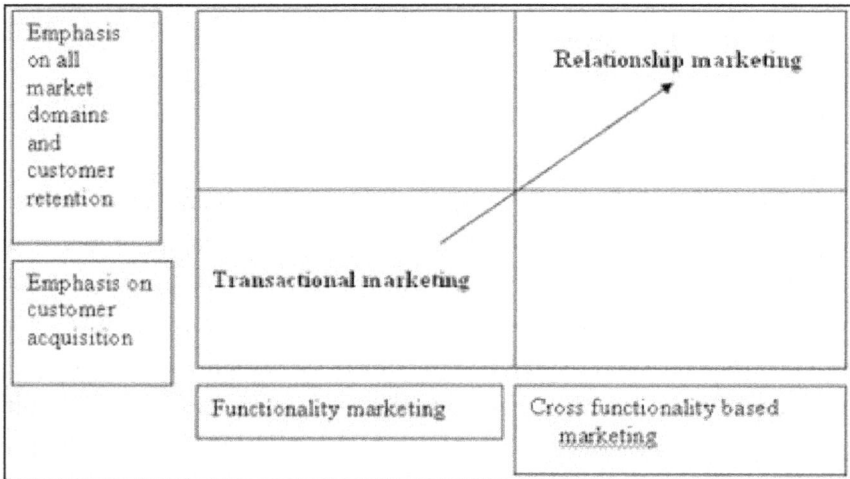

```
┌─────────────────────────────────────────────────────────────────┐
│ ┌──────────────┐┌──────────────────────┬──────────────────────┐ │
│ │ Emphasis     ││                      │                      │ │
│ │ on all       ││                      │  Relationship marketing │
│ │ market       ││                      │         ↗            │ │
│ │ domains      ││                      │       ↗              │ │
│ │ and          ││                      │     ↗                │ │
│ │ customer     ││                  ↗                          │ │
│ │ retention    ││                ↗                            │ │
│ └──────────────┘├──────────────┴──────────────────────────────┤ │
│ ┌──────────────┐│ Transactional marketing                     │ │
│ │ Emphasis on  ││                                             │ │
│ │ customer     ││                                             │ │
│ │ acquisition  ││                                             │ │
│ └──────────────┘└─────────────────────────────────────────────┘ │
│         ┌────────────────────────┐┌────────────────────────────┐ │
│         │ Functionality marketing ││ Cross functionality based  │ │
│         │                        ││        marketing           │ │
│         └────────────────────────┘└────────────────────────────┘ │
└─────────────────────────────────────────────────────────────────┘
```

4

Difference Between Transactional Marketing and Relationship Marketing

Essentially, transactional marketing focusses on getting the customer to buy a certain product and walk away, whilst relationship marketing sees the sale as the first step in the building of a relationship.

Transactional marketing stresses on immediate or one time purchase. It focusses strongly on the basic[4] marketing mix of price, promotion, physical distribution and product, and short-term benefits and product performance, with limited service. There is no concern about future exchanges, customer satisfaction, or customer loyalty to the business — it is all about delivering the functional components of value delivery. This type of marketing generates reactive relationships with the customers, and tends to be short-term in nature. M.W.Vilcox[5] says, "Transactional marketing focusses on maximising the profit of the company by recruiting more and more customers to purchase the firm's product." Relationship

4. Christopher Payne, *Relationship Marketing: Creating Shareholder Value*, Ballantyne.

5. M.W.Vilcox, *Contemporary Issues in Business Ethics*, Nova Science Publishers, Hauppauge, NY, 2007, 1-3. (ISBN 1-60021-773-7).

marketing is all about generating repeated sales and customer interactions, thus, focussing on bringing value creation, customer retention and long-term customer relations by providing and assuring long-term performance and service in all aspects. Relationship marketing reflects the need to create an integrated, cross-functional focus on collaboration. The focus is on emphasising customer retention and maximising the lifetime value of desired customer segments. The relationship marketing approach brings quality, customer service and marketing closely together.

In relationship marketing, the marketing customer does not merely buy a product, but instead buys a solution for a specific problem or need. And the company provides the customer with opportunities and benefits, not just the product as such. The goal of relationship marketing is customer delight whereas customer satisfaction is the goal of transactional marketing. Quality of production is given utmost importance in transaction marketing whereas quality in all aspects is given importance in relationship marketing. Two illustrative approaches to relationship marketing vs transaction approaches are Tesco and Wal-Mart. Whereas Tesco tries to engage in relationships with its local customers, resorting to loyalty programmes and such, Wal-Mart goes by the, "If you want loyalty, get a dog" motto, set by Sam Walton, and focusses on giving customers "Every day low prices", regardless of any past interactions. Buying a membership card in a supermarket is also an activity of sustaining the customers.

Methods of Building Relationship Marketing
Listen to customers' needs – Effective listening and providing undivided attention helps to build an effective relationship with the customers.

Anticipate customers' needs – Many customers are unable to identify and communicate their needs. Hence, the marketer should be wise enough to anticipate those unidentified needs.

Provide help to the customers – Take the advantage of helping them. Give them more than expected.

Apologise – The marketer should learn to apologise properly when he is not in a position to extend help.

Get feedback – Feedback is necessary to know the ultimate opinion on any task.

Build relationships – Build a relationship by repeated contacts, so that the customer can return for any further needs. This can be made possible through:

Face to face conversations.

Telephone conversations.

Creating goodwill.

Spending on valuable information like offers.

Mail campaigns.

Gifts.

Building Relationships Through Database Management

A database is the most important tool for customer relationship management The sales force keeps track of the customers and prospects, and plays a customer focussed role to retain customers. All customer relations are based on information, hospitality of the marketer, convenience or user friendly atmosphere, customer interest and customer interaction. Customer databases can be used for acquisition of customers, retention, and reacquisition (recovery of lost customers.

Advantages of database:

- Understanding customers and their prospects.
- Finding the key areas of interest
- Understanding the area of lacuna.
- Managing the competition.
- Managing the marketing communication system.

Creating a Customer Database

Setting up of a customer database is a priority task in any marketing organisation. But there are a few things to be considered before creating a database.

Data needed: Listing out all the data needed to be incorporated in the database.

Data collection: How to collect data? What are the sources of data collection?

Data storage: What are the various methods of storing the collected data?

Data usage: How are data retrieved and used effectively?

Data management: Who will handle the database? How much ease should the system provide the user?

Data upgrading: How feasible is to add or upgrade the database with a new system?

Scanner Data

All retail stores nowadays have created scanner data to find out the customer information and customer preference information. They provide this customer card to the frequent buyers. Offers on the point system are provided to the customers to motivate them to use the customer card. That is, their points will increase as per the purchase value. Various types of cards are provided to the customers, namely,

Proprietary credit card: Many retailers offer their own credit cards to study the customer's buying pattern.

Membership ID card: The retail house itself provides membership cards to its frequent buyers.

Credit Bureau's additional services: The customer's credit card gives reliable information about the customer's purchasing pattern. But it is difficult to get information through this method.

Creating a Database

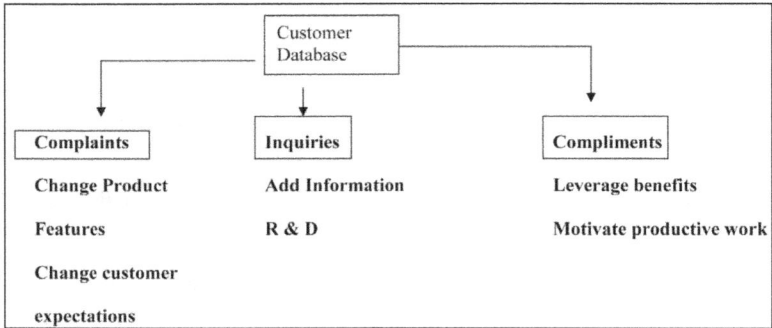

Tracking the customers is easy in certain areas like financial institutions: banks, brokers and insurance.

- Monopolies: public utilities and private monopolies.
- Contractual services.
- Personalised services.
- Retail stores.
- B2B companies...., etc.

Tracking the customers is difficult in certain areas:

- Restaurants, movies, dry cleaners.
- Small personal jobs.

Customer Reacquisition

Once lapsed, customers are identified and contacted for renewal of the relationship. They are mostly customers with a bad rapport. Hence, finding them and rectifying the mistakes that occurred should be done immediately. If the lapsed customer carries a good opinion, it is easy to renew the relationship, with more potential avenues.

Customer Relationship Management (CRM)

Definition

According to Business Dictionary.com, CRM means information-technology enabled strategy aimed at identifying, targeting, acquiring, and retaining the best mix of customers. CRM helps in profiling prospects, understanding their needs, and building relationships with them by providing the most-suitable products and a very high level of customer service. It integrates back and front office systems to create a database of customer contacts, purchases, information requested, technical support, etc. This database helps the firm in presenting a unified face to its customers, and also helps to improve the quality of the relationship. Though there are many ways to improve customer relationship, the most important factor is the satisfaction or dissatisfaction with the product / service offered by the company.

The diagram below (Fig 1) is the depiction of the CRM relationship in a marketing department. It shows how the three activities of the marketing department should work to accomplish the goals of the marketing department. This is applicable to both product-centric as well as service-centric organisations.

Fig 1

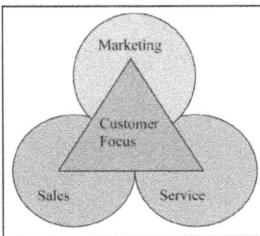

In the traditional marketing method, the 4 Ps of marketing, namely, Product, Price, Promotion and Physical distribution are given utmost importance and the customer is given less importance. But with the emergence of CRM, business has turned to customer-centric programmes. Customers can be satisfied by concentrating on three areas namely, sales, marketing and service.

There are three parts of the application architecture of CRM.

1. Operational CRM

Operational CRM means supporting the operations of the "front office" business processes which include customer contact (sales, marketing and service). Tasks resulting from these processes are forwarded to employees responsible for them. The information necessary for carrying out the tasks and interfaces to back-end applications is provided and activities with customers are documented for further reference. This has a direct dealing with the end user at the beginning stage itself, and interfaces and forwards the problem to the back end but does not deal with the problem later.

2. Analytical CRM

In analytical CRM, data gathered within the operational CRM are analysed to segment customers or to identify cross- and up-selling potential. Data collection and analysis is viewed as a continuing and perpetual process. At every perpetual cycle, business decisions are refined over time, based on feedback from earlier analyses and decisions. Apart from this, with the aid of system-based business intelligence, many types of CRM software are available, based on functionality like front-end user and back-end user and also as integrated system application software.

3. Collaborative CRM

Collaborative CRM facilitates interactions with customers through all channels (personal, letter, fax, phone, web, e-mail) and supports co-ordination of employee teams and channels. It is a solution that brings people, processes and data together so that companies can better serve and retain their customers. The data/activities can be structured, unstructured, conversational, and/or transactional, disguised or undisguised in nature.

Merits of relationship marketing:

- Emphasis on relationship rather than a transactional approach to marketing.
- Projecting a positive image of the organisation among the consumers.
- Extending the principles of relationship marketing in order to enter the diverse market domains.

- Building goodwill in the market.
- Improving customer satisfaction.
- Enhancing brand equity through customer retention and loyalty.
- Maintaining parity between the internal market within the organisation as well as with external relationship variables like customers, suppliers, referral sources, etc.
- Creating cooperative and collaborative activities that aim to enhance the mutual economic value of both the marketer and customer at reduced cost.

In the book *Ageless Marketing*[6], relationship marketing is considered as ageless marketing. It is a strategic means for extending a brand's reach based on the principles of Developmental Relationship Marketing (DRM). DRM is a marketing platform that integrates stage-of-life changes in needs and behaviour with recent and often astonishing findings in brain research concerning how our brains detect and react to incoming information and how our conscious minds form perceptions, thoughts and decisions. Ageless marketing is just one strategy in these challenging times. DRM relies on research, developmental psychology, and, most importantly, a client's values and views.

Relationship marketing is an extension of database marketing. Instead of targeting anonymous customers, customers are personalised and identified by name. Customers are won over by dialogue and by creation of trust which leads to customer retention. The relationship should be mutually beneficial. It is a win-win strategy.

But Alan Mitchell[7] in his book *Right Side Up* says it has a negative side which he refers to as slug trail marketing and customer stalking. According to him, practically, it is not a win-win strategy, just piling up of data bases and calling them for relationships repeatedly whether

---

6. David B. Wolfe, Robert E. Snyder, *Ageless Marketing: Strategies For Reaching The Hearts And Minds Of The New Customer Majority*, Dearborn Trade, p. 359.
7. Alan Mitchel, *Right Side Up*, Harper Collins Business.

they need it or not. It is just like hitting repeatedly to retain them. Many of the customers do not like a relationship with the seller except in case they need after sales service. And moreover, customers are treated as experiment rats. They are repeatedly checked with stimulus response to find out which stimulus makes them respond. This does not help to build a relationship. It results in fighting back by the customers.

The Six Markets Model

Christopher, Payne and Ballantyne (1991) from Cranfield[8] University have identified six markets that are central to relationship marketing. These are:

Internal markets – This is the market in which buying and selling of goods takes place within the organisation. Example: Government companies which purchase from other similar outlets and the European market, where there is single pricing for buying and selling of goods throughout the countries of the European Union (EU).

Supplier markets – In this market, suppliers are included as marketing partners.

Recruitment markets – The employee is considered a strong marketing force. And, hence, recruiting the right person for the right job is a crucial task in marketing.

Referral markets - Referral marketing is developing and implementing a marketing plan to stimulate referrals by best use of the resources.

Influence markets - This involves a wide range of sub-markets, including: government regulators, standards bodies, lobbyists, stockholders, bankers, venture capitalists, financial analysts, stockbrokers, consumer associations, environmental associations, and labour associations that have the potential to influence people.

Customer markets – There are customers and consumers in this market. Customers are often intermediaries, distributors and retailers. Whereas consumers are end-users.

---

8. M. Christopher, A. Payne and Ballentyne, *Relationship Marketing*, second edition, (Oxford: Butterworth-Heinemann, 2001).

Types of Relationship Marketing

Three types of relationship marketing programmes are followed by corporates. These are:

Continuity marketing : This is about continually building relationships by special supply chain arrangements.

Individual marketing: This is about marketing to the individual customers by creating loyalty.

Co- marketing / partnering marketing: This is marketing through co-branding, cooperative methods.

Customer Reacquisition

Permission marketing (also called invitational marketing / opt-in marketing/ privacy marketing).

Freedom is coming to mean little more than the right to ask permission.

— Joseph Sobran

Definition

Marketing centred on obtaining customer consent to receive information from a company.

Seth Godin[9] (1999) has coined and proposed a new idea: permission marketing. The idea is to understand the lifetime value of the customer and allocate resources in accordance with these values. The emphasis is on retaining existing customers rather than obtaining new ones. In the words of Seth Godin, "Turning strangers into friends, and friends into customers." One should get into the customer need by asking, "May I?"

What is Permission Marketing?

Permission marketing motivates customers and prospects to agree and receive marketing communication messages. It offer consumers the

---

9. Seth Godin, *Permission Marketing*, Simon & Schuster, 1999.

opportunity to voluntarily receive marketing materials via e-mail or through other modes of communication

In the words of Seth Godin, "Turning strangers into friends, and friends into customers."

Advertisements don't work like they did earlier as people have got used to them and the impact is less. Hence, there is a need for something that can fulfill the requirements of the customer rather than interrupting a reluctant customer. Permission marketing is said to be anticipated, personal and relevant. Anticipated because people actually look forward to seeing the information. Personal because the messages are directly related to the individual. Relevant because the marketing is about something the prospect is interested in. The opposite terminology of permission marketing is the traditional interruption marketing. Instead of fighting for the attention of mass customers by advertising to the masses and interrupting them, it is always better to personalise and market to their needs.

Permission marketing works face-to-face, over the telephone, through the post, and in points-based systems. But it is revolutionised when used with e-mail and the Internet where the costs of reach and frequency as well as production are substantially reduced. Permission marketing can be introduced to customers through the following methods:

- Online permission marketing.
- Offline permission marketing medium.
- Coupons, sweepstakes and promotional offers.
- Warranty cards.
- Membership and frequent-buyer clubs.
- Catalogues.
- Toll-free numbers.
- Surveys.

Permission Marketing and the Internet
Cyber traffic is a big problem for Internet users. This increases the

search cost for the customers. Moreover, pages that are not updated, which are called debris, also increase the cost. Though there are many search engines, the debris and cyber traffic cause hindrance in reaching the customers. Search engines help customers to navigate, to look for sites that are in the list or look through only a few pages. They do not navigate through 14 or 15 pages. Hence, it is better to personalise through permission marketing.

Any type of Internet advertising feedback is hard to measure. Many permission-marketing firms (e.g. yesmail.com- now part of the business incubator, CMGI) claim customer response rates in terms of geographical location. Since the ads arrive in the mailbox of the individual, it is likely that more attention would be paid to them in comparison to banners.

Even though permission marketing can be implemented in any direct medium, it has emerged as a serious idea only with the advent of the Internet. The two reasons for this are:

- The cost of b2c communication is low.
- The Internet has enabled rapid feedback mechanisms due to instantaneous two-way communication.
- Another motivation for permission marketing on the Web has been the failure of the direct mail approach of sending unsolicited promotional messages. The prime example of this is unsolicited commercial e-mail or "Spam" (Cranor & LaMacchia, 1998).
- Reaching target customers directly.
- Easy to create database of interested customers and targeting it.

Permission marketing has now become a large-scale activity on the Internet. Permission marketing models allow for two kinds of exit or opt-out strategies: partial or complete. In partial opt-out, the consumer indicates that he or she wants to stop receiving advertisements in a sub-category. For example, this may occur when the consumer is interested in a category for a short period of time only. New models now allow consumers to specify a date after which they will be automatically opted out of a category. In complete opt-out, the consumer decides to terminate a relationship with a particular marketer and, hence, will not receive any more promotional messages. Permission marketing allows customer to volunteer by responding to the permission.

Seth Godin explains the six levels of permission marketing
(in descending order of impact):

Intravenous Treatment
When the customers give permission to the marketer to take decisions, it is termed intravenous treatment. This happens when the customer trusts his marketer, or when the customer is totally confused on product details. It saves the time and money of the customer. For example, a doctor treating a patient in the emergency room doesn't have to sell very hard while administering a drug. Hence, the needed service is easily administered to the people who need it.

Green Stamps
Executives suffer through long layovers to gain frequent-flyer miles. Here, the company rewards customers in a currency they care about. They give points for customers' loyalty and provide them gifts. Credit card companies and supermarkets provide points for the purchases that consumers make. The points are scalable and, hence, a strong line of loyalty can be drawn.

Personal Relationships
The nearby shop is always preferred if the customer's need is fulfilled there. A favourite retailer can "upscale" you (recommend something more expensive) without offending you.

Branding
Given a choice between the known and the unknown, most people choose the known.

Situational Selling
A customer in the store who is about to make a purchase, often welcomes unsolicited marketing advice. Advice from the shopkeeper is valued more.

Spam
Where most marketers live most of the time: calling a stranger — at home, during dinner, without permission. Most of the marketing methods are spam.

Seth Godwin in his book *Permission Marketing* talks about 8 keys of permission marketing

Strategy: Whether complete or partial opt-ins should be used.

Technology: Use of technology and content according to desire.

Permission: Getting permission from the customer for further contacts.

Trust: Making use of captured permission to build trust.

Media: Most customers prefer e-mail as it works out cheaper.

Content: As most customers have spam, it is necessary to work on contents in an attractive manner.

Link to commerce: Fulfilling the business practically.

Measurement: By back-tracking customers who enquire, the database can be created and measured.

Fig 2

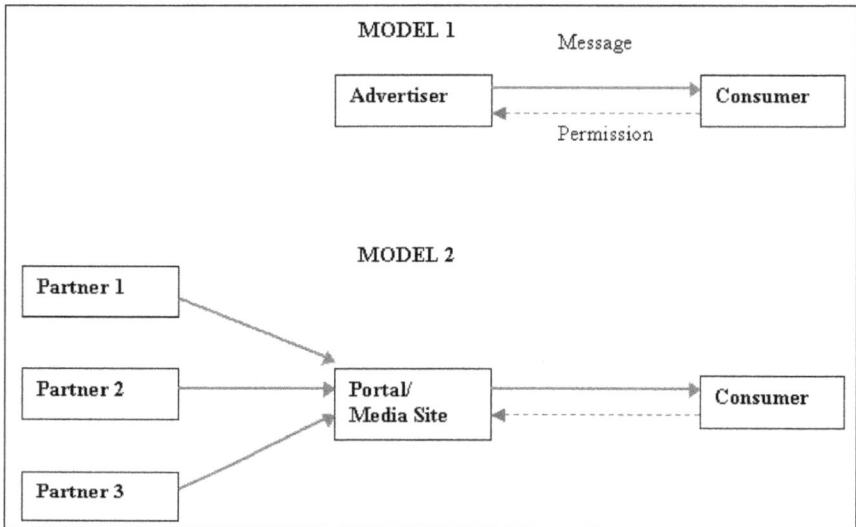

Source: http://jcmc.indiana.edu/vol6/issue2/krishnamurthy.html

Current Practice of Permission Marketing: Four Business Models

Model 1 is the depiction of direct relationship maintenance. Here, the advertiser has direct contact with the customer and he knows that his customers are in need of the information which he intends to provide. This is characterised by low permission intensity, direct contact with the advertiser and minimal targeting.

Model 2 can be described as a permission partnership. Here, the consumer provides a portal or media site with the permission to send him or her promotional offers. After receiving this permission, the intermediary alerts its partners who wish to send out promotional offers. All consumers signed on receive all the offers. Examples of this include nytimes.com and lycos.com. This is commonly used to increase traffic to websites. Hence, here we have low to medium permission intensity, contact through an intermediary and low targeting.

Fig 3

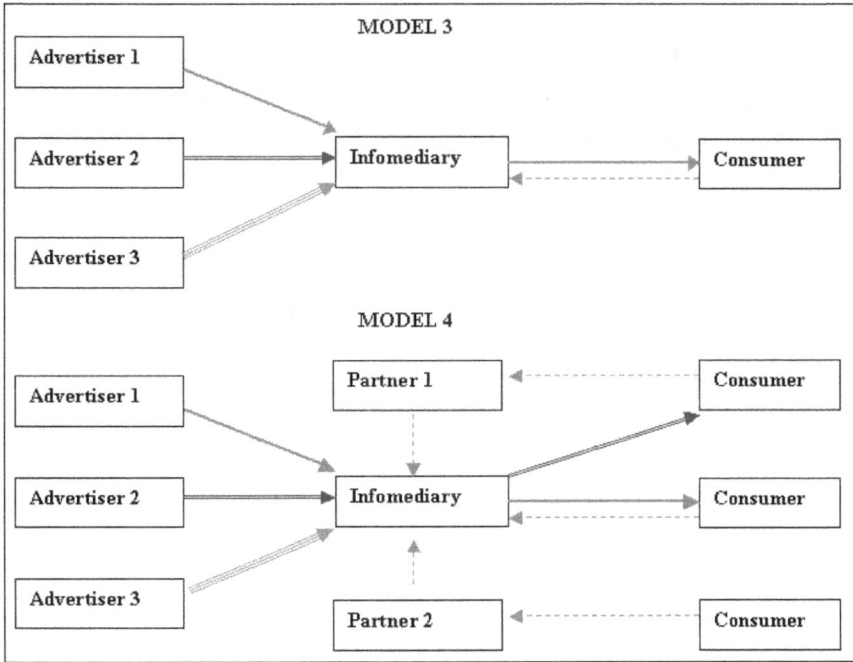

MODEL 3

Advertiser 1 · Advertiser 2 · Advertiser 3 → Infomediary → Consumer

MODEL 4

Advertiser 1 · Advertiser 2 · Advertiser 3 → Infomediary → Consumer; Partner 1 · Partner 2 ← Consumer

Source: http://jcmc.indiana.edu/vol6/issue2/krishnamurthy.html

Model 3 can be described as an ad market. A consumer provides an infomediary[10] with detailed information about his or her preferences and interests. The infomediary then uses this information to identify advertisers. An infomediary is a person who works as a personal agent on behalf of consumers to help them take control over information gathered about them for use by marketers and advertisers. The concept of the infomediary was first suggested by the McKinsey consultants, Professors John Hagel III, and Marc Singer. The ads supplied by these advertisers are then carefully targeted at the consumers. Advertisers find target customers for their promotions with lower cost of targeting and the infomediary makes a profit by facilitating this exchange. Hence, there is high permission intensity, contact through an infomediary and the potential for high targeting precision.

10. John Hagel III and Marc Singer, *Net Worth,* Harvard Business School Press, ISBN -0-87584-889-3, 1999.

Model 4 can be termed as a permission pool. Here, different consumers provide different firms with the permission to send them promotional offers. The advertisers pool out various firms' information to the consumers and then promotional messages are sent out targeting the larger pool of customers for every product. Examples of this practice include yesmail.com.

CHAPTER 5

Social and Societal
Marketing Techniques

How can a society that exists on instant mashed potatoes, packaged cake
mixes, frozen dinners, and instant cameras teach patience to its young?
— Paul Sweeney

Social and Societal Marketing

Society is a system that provides a healthy environment to all living beings.
It is web of social relationships which are changing. Due to innumerable
of interactions on social grounds, social issues emerge. These social issues
need solutions. For reaching solutions, people need an aid, which may
be a product or a service. Hence, there is a wide opportunity to market
these necessary products/ services.

There are so many social issues to which companies can help bring
awareness through their marketing, company image and their product
influence in society. These companies should consider this as their
corporate responsibility and help in bringing change for the common
good.

Difference Between Social Marketing and Societal Marketing

When a company brings about awareness about a social issue, it is called social marketing. Such social advertisements and other promotional tools should be creative and emotionally touching as the benefit is less to the individual and more to society as a whole. It should reach, and appeal to, individual minds.

When a company follows certain production processes that promote the well-being of society, it is referred to as societal marketing.

Social Issues

Some social issues that are in the priority list are as under:

Demarketing child labour.

Funding children's education.

Saving the environment.

Go Green — stop killing animals.

Save animals that are on the verge of extinction – save the panda, tiger, etc.

Save the earth programmes.

Awareness on AIDS.

Afforestation.

Save natural resources.

Sanitation.

Examples of Social Advertisements by Companies

- Tata Tea, during the election period, urged people to vote and become responsible citizens.
- Idea, the mobile SIM card company, advertised for, "Save Paper" in a campaign which features Hindi movie actor Abhishek Bachchan. He won the best brand ambassador award of the year 2007.

Many television programmes are based on social causes. For example, NDTV's environment reality show Lead India, Tech India, Aap ki Adaalat, etc.

Social Advertising

This promotes social issues by both profit and non-profit organisations for their goods or services. It aims to create mass awareness and has wide recall for a longer period of time. It involves bringing about attitudinal change on social issues.

The effect of social advertising is not immediate. It can happen slowly and steadily over the years. The result should be predicted on a long-term basis.

Fig 1

Source: wikipedia commonos

Fig 2

Source: wikipedia commonos

Fig 3

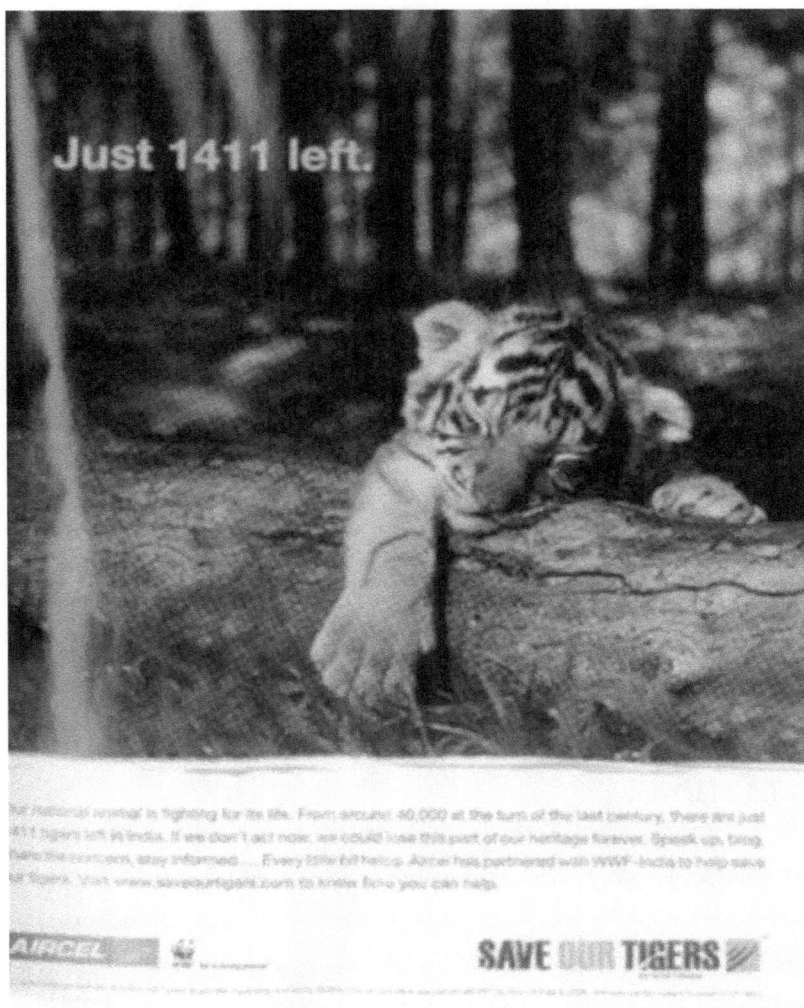

The advertisement above is from the Government of India to save tigers from extinction.

Source: Femina/March 10, 2010/p. 95.

Fig 4

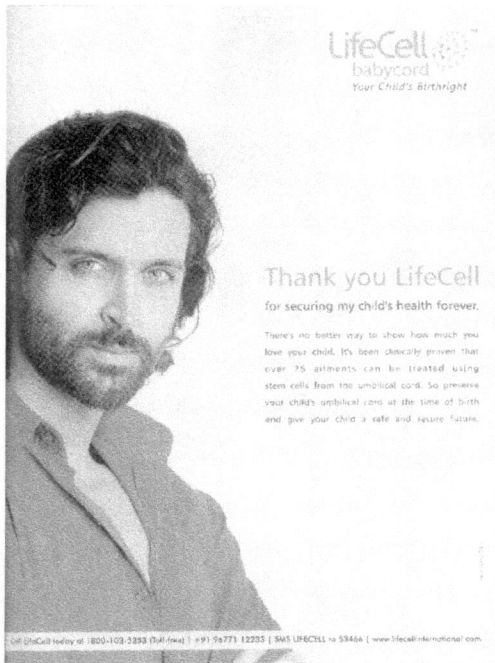

Source: Femina/March 10, 2010/p .95.

Societal Marketing

As we advance in life, we learn the limits of our abilities.

— Henry Ford

The societal marketing concept is an enlightened one that holds that a company should make good marketing decisions by considering the consumer's wants, the company's requirements, and the society's long-term interests. It is closely linked with the principles of corporate social responsibility and sustainable development.

The concept lays emphasis on social responsibility and suggests that for a company to only focus on an exchange relationship with customers might not be suitable in order to sustain long-term success. Rather, the marketing strategy should deliver value to customers in a way that maintains or improves both the consumer's and the society's well-being.

Most companies recognise that socially responsible activities improve their image among customers, stockholders, the financial community, and other relevant members of the public. Ethical and socially responsible practices are simply good business, resulting not only in a favourable image, but ultimately in increased sales.

Societal marketing is basically a marketing concept that is of the view that a company must make good marketing decisions after considering the consumer's wants, the requirements of the company and, most of all, the long-term interests of the society.

Societal marketing is actually an offshoot of the concept of corporate social responsibility and sustainable development. This concept urges companies to do more than having an exchange relationship with customers, to go beyond delivering products, and work for the benefit of the consumers and the society.

Green marketing refers to the process of selling products and/or services based on their environmental benefits. Such a product or service may be environmentally friendly in itself or produced and/or packaged in an environmentally friendly way. It is also referred to as environmental marketing, ecological marketing, eco-marketing.

The American Marketing Association (AMA) defines green marketing in three ways:

- The marketing of products that are presumed to be environmentally safe (retailing definition).
- The development and marketing of products designed to minimise negative effects on the physical environment or to improve its quality (social marketing definition).
- The efforts by organisations to produce, promote, package, and reclaim products in a manner that is sensitive or responsive to ecological concerns (environmental definition).

Examples

The following are three examples of the societal marketing concept:

- **Navaneet Publications (India) Limited**: They manufacture ecobuddy notebooks from bagasse (leftover sugarcane pulp) instead of wood pulp. These are ecofriendly notebooks as they save on cutting down of trees for paper.
- **Ariel:** Ariel is a detergent manufactured by Procter and Gamble. Ariel runs special fund raising campaigns for the deprived classes of the world, specifically in the developing countries. It also contributes part of its profits from every bag sold for the development of the society.
- **Indian Tobacco Corporation (ITC):** The company has reduced the production of cigarettes and diversified into the area of biscuit manufacturing in the brand name Sunfeast.
- **Lifebouy**: When the people of North Indian states suffered from cholera due to unhygienic ways of sanitation, Lifebouy educated the villagers about the importance of cleanliness, pure drinking water and following clean habits like washing hands with soap, keeping food and water in closed containers, etc. and marketed their handwash and soap by providing free samples in the disease hit areas.
- **Proctor & Gamble** introduced a brand of fat free oil to prevent the growing incidence of heart disease.
- Various automobile manufacturers are focussing more on producing CNG cars that are not only environment friendly but also economical. This trend is gaining popularity. One can verify it by observing the increasing number of CNG stations.
- Various companies are favouring the use of recycled paper in order to save trees.
- Many automobile companies are making mini e-cars which are less polluting for the environment than petrol cars. Nissan Mo introduced a non-emission car by the name 'Leaf'. Ford Focus is another environment friendly car. Other companies like Fisker Automotive,

Aperta Motors and Coda are launching their electric cars in the international market.

- **Philips launched the CFL (candescent fluorescent lamp)** in 1994 which is environment friendly and an energy saving device. As it was not compatible with old type fixtures, it was a failure. Later, Philips reintroduced it, with successful modulations.
- **Green Credentials** : Natural association between the environmentally friendly nature of the sport (only wind power used, except in case of an emergency), and in-port racing and Volvo cars designed with greater energy efficiency and less environmental impact.
- **Cause Related Marketing/ Sponsorship (CRM):** Cause related marketing is a partnership between a for-profit company and a non-profit organisation, which increases a company's sales, has a positive impact on the brand or corporate image, while raising money and visibility for the cause. Example: Tesco "Free computers for schools"; Shakthi Masala giving employment opportunities for physically challenged people.

Limitations

Societal marketing sidesteps the potential conflict among customer wants, company interests and long-run societal welfare.

Societal marketing should not be confused with social marketing. The societal marketing concept was a forerunner of sustainable marketing in integrating issues of social responsibility into commercial marketing strategies. In contrast, social marketing applies commercial marketing theories, tools and techniques to social issues. Social marketing uses a "customer orientated" approach and applies the concepts and tools used by commercial marketers in pursuit of social goals like anti-smoking-campaigns or fund raising for NGOs.

Fig 5

Source: Outlook Business /Special issue/December 12, 2009, Pg. Cover).

Advantages

- It is a social responsibility.
- Cost factors are reduced.
- Recycling of products is often done.
- It is customer's right to get harmless products.

Disadvantages

- *Greenwashing* is any form of marketing or public relations that links a corporate, political, religious or non-profit organisation to a positive association with environmental issues for an unsustainable product, service, or practice. It is an eye-wash for green products. Greenwashing was a term coined by NY environmentalist Jay Westerveld, in 1986, in an essay regarding the hotel industry's practice of placing green placards in each room, promoting reuse of guest-towels, ostensibly to "save the environment".

- It is a highly dangerous method when it becomes greenwash to build a brand image which is not true or ethical.

CHAPTER 6

Integrated or Fusion and Neuromarketing

Integrated Marketing (IM) / Fusion Marketing

You don't understand anything until you learn it more than one way.
— Marvin Minsky

Integrated Marketing (IM) is a management strategy and meta-discipline focussed on the organisation-wide optimisation of unique values for the stakeholder. It is a holistic approach.

It is marketing characterised by the systematic and simultaneous integration, planning, and development of marketing activities implemented by a company over time:

- When there is a large number of customers.
- The media are fragmented.
- Mass interest is also fragmented.
- Improper communication strategy.

- Heavy competition.
- Manifold reach.
- Even if one method of marketing fails, another one could catch up with the market.

Integrated marketing can be achieved only through integrated marketing communication. Every company communicates via more than one media, say, through mail and telephone, which is commonly done. Now, it is a strategic decision to take into account many modes of communication realising the split in the target group. Nowadays, one company targets different segments of people as they produce many models of the product to satisfy all categories of buyers. There is a need for many modes of communication to reach out to many categories of buyers. Unintegrated communications send disjointed messages which dilute the impact of the message. This may also confuse, frustrate and arouse anxiety in customers. On the other hand, integrated communications present a reassuring sense of order.

Integrated marketing is defined as a concept of marketing communications planning that recognises the added value of a comprehensive plan that evaluates the strategic roles of a variety of communication disciplines and combines these disciplines to provide clarity, consistency and maximum communications impact. It involves a synergistic approach to achieving the objectives of a marketing campaign. While deciding on various marketing techniques, the marketing mix and product life-cycle should be kept in mind.

Why do companies go for the Integrated Marketing Communications (IMC) approach?

- Synergy (the whole is greater than the sum of the parts) / cost saving/ less duplication.
- Differentiates from the competition.
- Brings greater accountability.
- Provides internal focus.

- Greater impact / cuts through clutter.
- Efficient and effective marketing communication programmes.
- Globalisation.
- Move from transactional to relationship marketing.
- Fragmentation of traditional media.
- Cynicism towards traditional communication techniques.
- Intense competition.

Integrated Marketing Communications (IMC) is a term used to describe a holistic approach to marketing communication. It aims to ensure consistency of the message and the complementary use of the media. The concept includes online and offline marketing channels.

- **Direct selling**: It is a retail service through the proper channel of distribution. It works through direct personal presentation, demonstration, and sale of products and services to consumers, usually in their homes or at their jobs. It is often made in first time as well as repeat purchases. There are certain advantages like personal demonstration, home delivery, explanations. It is considered as the best way of doing business, socialising with the customers, and allows flexi-time business. It is a cost-effective channel of marketing. There are two types of direct selling, namely,
  Single layer direct selling – Where the seller and buyer meet directly and the process of selling is very easy.
  Multi-layer selling –It is like multi-level marketing where many people together sell the product. Direct selling has location limitations whereas multi-level marketing does not have that limitation. Direct selling does not require the recruiting of more salespersons.
- **Personal selling**: At point of purchase.

Personal selling is a promotional method in which one party (e.g., salesperson) uses skills and techniques for building personal relationships with another party (e.g., those involved in a purchase decision) that results in both parties obtaining value. In most cases, the "value" for the salesperson is realised through the financial rewards of the sale while the customer's "value" is realised from the benefits obtained by use of the product. Because selling involves personal contact, this promotional method often works through face-to-face meetings or via a telephone conversation, though newer technologies allow contact to take place over the Internet, including using video conferencing or text messaging (e.g. online chat).

- **Telemarketing** : This is the business or practice of marketing goods or services over the telephone. Some people believe that in the 1950s, DialAmerica Marketing, Inc became the first company completely dedicated to inbound and outbound telephone sales and services. The company, spun-off and sold by Time, Inc. magazine in 1976, became the largest provider of telephone sales and services to magazine publishing companies. The term *telemarketing* was first used extensively in the late 1970s to describe Bell Systems communications which related to new uses for the outbound WATS and inbound toll-free services
  - **Outbound** is proactive marketing in which prospective and preexisting customers are contacted directly. In this method, the company takes the initiatives of reaching the customer.
  - **Inbound** is a reactive reception of incoming orders and requests for information. Demand is generally created by advertising, publicity, or the efforts of outside salespeople. Here, the customer takes the initiative of reaching the company.

Prospective customers are identified by various means, including past purchase history, previous requests for information, credit limit, competition entry forms, and application forms. Names may also be purchased from another company's consumer database or obtained from a telephone directory or any other public list. The qualification process is intended to determine which customers are most likely to purchase the product or service. Telemarketing techniques are also applied to other forms of electronic marketing using e-mail or fax messages, in which case they are frequently considered spam by some people.

Fraudulent telemarketing companies are frequently referred to as "telemarketing boiler rooms" or simply "boiler rooms." Telemarketing is often criticised as an unethical business practice due to the perception of high-pressure sales techniques during unsolicited calls. Telemarketers marketing telephone companies may participate in telephone slamming, the practice of switching off a customer's telephone service without their knowledge or authorisation.

- **Multimedia**: This is the combination of audio and video services and devices. There are three types, namely, streaming audio/video, streaming live audio/video and interactive audio/video. Streaming means the user or customer can listen or watch on demand. An example is the telecast of a film song in a television soap. Streaming live audio video means broadcasting radio and television programmes through the Internet. Example: Internet teleconference. Interactive audio video refers to the use of the Internet for interactive applications.
- **Events**: Seminars, speeches, trade shows, events, etc. represent a significant opportunity to enhance brand and product visibility, promote new and existing products, generate leads and drive meaningful sales.

In addition, show participation enables the customer to learn about industry trends, gain competitor insights, make key industry contacts, and further solidify relationships with current customers.

- Generating sales leads.
- Generating actual sales at the show.
- Enhancing your image and visibility.
- Reaching a specific audience.
- Establishing a presence in the marketplace.

- Improving the effectiveness and efficiency of marketing efforts.
- Personally meeting customers, competitors and suppliers.
- Prospecting for new customers.
- Introducing new products and services.
- Demonstrating a product in ways not possible using other marketing channels.
- Recruiting distributors or dealers.
- Educating the target audience.

Virtual trade shows: These are nothing but online trade shows.

Online trade is economical. It has no costs for transportation, shipping, hotels, hospitality, or booths, and just a minimal cost for the exhibiting space.

Eco-friendly: Compared to traditional trade shows, virtual trade shows are "greener." Lowering the environmental impact is an increasingly important goal for many companies. Tax incentives for cutting fuel costs are also likely to increase, making virtual exhibits an even more attractive proposition.

Lead generation: Virtual trade shows collect the data for you, and most include built-in lead management software. Suddenly, tracking those leads becomes simple. In addition, many systems offer tags so you can make notes on attendees or companies, making it easy to follow up. You can also keep tabs on both staff and attendee activities.

Though it is not a popular method, the early marketer will attract more customers. The wise marketing professional will use this exciting new technology to reach out to customers.

- **Internet/Website** – e-mail drip marketing, banners, blogs, search engines etc.
- **Networking** – Meeting and greeting people is the foundation for business.

Bluetooth is a wireless LAN technology designed to connect devices of different functions such as the telephone, computer, laptop, camera, printer, mobile, etc. Bluethooth can be connected to the Internet. The bluetooth network is called the piconet which is made up of eight stations, namely one primary station and all other secondary stations. Piconets are combined to form the scatternet.

Advantages of Piconet
- It is used to operate wireless devices like the wireless mouse, keyboard, etc.
- It is often used in sensory devices. Hence, it has wide application in health care systems, automatic doors and hand wash taps, forensic science and espionage systems.
- Satellite network: It is the combination of nodes, some of which are satellites, that provide communication from one point on the earth to another. It has very high quality communication that can be used to reach even remote and underdeveloped areas on the earth.

- **Paid Advertising**: Newspapers, journals, radio, television, including cable, and sponsorships at silent auctions are all examples of paid advertising.
- **Professionalism**: The business card is one of the most valuable networking tools that can increase business referrals. The business card is energy-efficient, low-cost, low-tech, and keeps working for you hours, weeks and even years after it is handed out.
- **Promotional Items**: Promotional products include merchandise items, corporate gifts, or any product that can be imprinted with your company logo for promotional use, including calendars, DVDs, pens, pencils, key rings or even stress balls.

Advantages of Using Promotional Products
- *Flexible:* promotional products can be used in all situations, from a corporate uniform to business gifts, or even merchandise.
- *Tangible and long-lasting*: promotional products have the benefit of

being a long-lasting form of marketing. They are not limited to the life of a magazine or newspaper.

- *Impact and effectiveness* can be easily measured: the success of using promotional products in your marketing campaigns is easily measured, with obvious results every time.
- *Higher perceived value*: promotional products have a higher perceived value, so when your clients/potential clients receive a promotional product, they feel they are important to your company or organisation.
- *Complements targeted marketing campaigns:* promotional products complement targeted marketing campaigns, with the ability to be themed and customised to a specific campaign. *Complements other advertising methods*: promotional products work effectively when combined with other advertising media, increasing response rates and the overall effectiveness of the advertising media.

Disadvantages
- Scalability or measurability of each medium.
- Differentiated services are hard to access.

Integrated marketing is classified into two types.
- Combination of simple promotional tools.
- Comprehensive programmes used as marketing promotional tools (this has specialised appeal to special audience).

There are two types of information processing.
- Replacement model.
- Accumulation model.

In the replacement model, the company can replace the existing image and try to build a better one. Whereas in the accumulation model, the various forms of promotion will help the customers to store information in their minds which will help to form an idea about the company, product and brand. This will help to retrieve their memory at the point of purchase.

Stages of Purchase

IMC helps customers to move through the various stages of the buying process. At every stage of purchase, different types of promotion should be used. Hence, it should be thoroughly analysed as to who is the customer and which stage he belongs to before communicating with him. The organisation simultaneously consolidates its image, develops a dialogue and nurtures its relationship with customers.

The American Association of Advertising Agencies (the "4As") developed one of the first definitions of integrated marketing communications: a concept of marketing communications planning that recognises the added value of a comprehensive plan that evaluates the strategic roles of a variety of communication disciplines— for example, general advertising, direct response, sales promotion, and public relations—and combines these disciplines to provide clarity, consistency, and maximum communications impact.

The 4As definition focusses on the process of using all forms of promotion.

There are three stages of purchase where IMC is most required.

Pre-purchase stage: Where the need of advertisement is high. Information about the product will build brand image and the customer will decide about the brand.

Purchase stage: Direct selling plays a major role. Improper communication from the salesperson or unavailability of the product may distract the purchase decision.

Post purchase stage: Good relations with the customer and after sales service will bring in new customers. Advertisements will help to reduce post purchase anxiety.

Drip Marketing

Drip marketing involves a carefully planned and thoughtfully targeted series of communications that will get your message across to customers and keep your company's name in their minds. As prospects move through the early stages of the sell cycle, drip marketing helps to ensure that those potential customers become your actual customers.

Advantages

- Building awareness is one of the most important advantages of drip marketing. It fixes your company name and message in the potential customer's mind.
- It is a form of adaptation to customer preference and taste.
- Internet marketing can be considered not only as a promotional tool but also as a communicative medium since it is interactive.
- There is a synergy in the overall promotion.
- Education is another important function. Drip marketing can inform prospects about your products and your industry by giving useful information while building trust in your company.
- Drip marketing is ideal for high-value products with a long sell cycle, especially high-ticket items which are purchased at infrequent intervals.
- Drip marketing needs careful planning for maximum effect.

In order to reach a better understanding of the full meaning and process of IMC, Smith et al. (1999) have developed a tool which is supposed to show marketing integration as occurring at one or more of seven levels. They distinguish the following levels and corresponding degrees of integration.

- *Vertical objectives integration:* It means that communication objectives fit with marketing objectives and the overall corporate objectives. Modes of communication should correspond with, and respond to, the organisational objectives.
- *Horizontal/functional integration:* Marketing communications

activities should fulfill the function or other departmental objectives.

- *Marketing mix integration:* The marketing mix of product, price and place decisions is consistent with the promotion decisions, e.g. with the required communication messages.
- *Communications mix integration:* All the communications tools should guide the customer/consumer/client through each stage of the buying process.
- *Creative design integration:* The creative design and execution is uniform and consistent with the chosen positioning of the product.
- *Internal/external integration:* All internal departments and all external employed agencies are working together to an agreed plan and strategy. The communication is vertical as well as horizontal
- *Financial integration:* The budget is used in the most effective and efficient way, ensuring that economies of scale are achieved and long-term investment is optimised.

Communication is the process by which individuals share meaning. This means that each participant must fully understand the meaning of the other's communication. Otherwise, no dialogue will occur. Only through knowledge and understanding of the communication process are the actors likely to achieve their objectives of influencing attitudes, knowledge and/or behaviour to persuade, which is one of the most prominent reasons why organisations need to communicate (Fill, 1999). With increasing worldwide interest in the emergent concept and field of IMC, it is important to investigate its theoretical foundations.

Shannon and Weaver (1949) noticed that recent years had witnessed considerable research activity in communication theory. They stated that the fundamental problem of communication is that of reproducing at one point, either exactly or approximately, a message selected at another point (Shannon and Weaver, 1949, p. 3). By a communication system, Shannon and Weaver meant a system comprising essentially five parts:

- An information source which produces a message or sequence of messages to be communicated to a receiving terminal. The messages may be of various types.
- A transmitter which operates on the message to produce a signal suitable for transmission over the channel.
- The channel is merely the medium used to transmit the signal from the transmitter to the receiver.
- The receiver reconstructs the message from the signal.
- The destination is the person for whom the message is intended.

It is a matter of common interest for academics, professional schools and practitioners at strategic and tactical levels to close the gap in order to move IMC from tactics to strategy. This can be achieved by international research and reconsidering educational programmes regarding management, and marketing communications. According to the Shannon and Weaver Model of Communication, any message is transmitted through the encoder, signals are sent through a channel, and decoded as a message. But it has to undergo disturbance or interference in transmission, which is called noise.

Fig 1: Schematic Diagram of a General Communication System

The Shannon-Weaver Mathematical Model, 1949

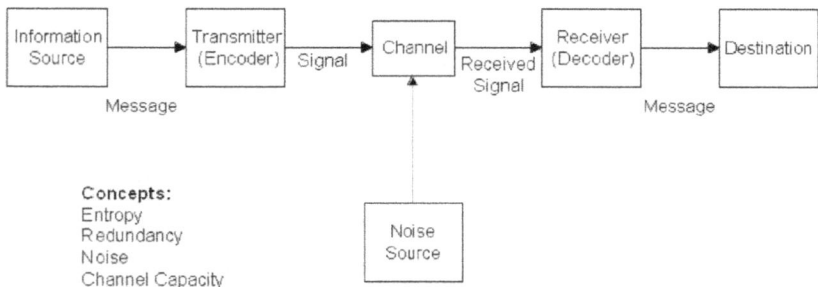

Source: www.shkaminski.com/.../Communication%20**Models**.htm

Neuromarketing

I washed your brain, but I had trouble getting the think stains out.
— Cindy (character in *The Adventures of Jimmy Neutron:*
Boy Genius, 2002)

Neuromarketing is a new form of marketing research that combines the techniques of neuroscience and clinical psychology to develop insights into how we respond to products, brands, and advertisements. Nueuromarketing helps to discover the buy button in business; it is the study of the brain's responses to advertising, to the brands encountered in our daily lives.

Gary Zaltman, a professor at Harvard University, is the father of neuromarketing. In 1994, along with his friends, he scanned the brains of consumers to find out their buying behaviour. "The father of neuromarketing, Professor Ale Smidts, winner of the Nobel Prize for Economy in 2002, says the term neuromarketing, that was created in the same year, 2002, designates the use of identification techniques of cerebral mechanisms to understand the consumer's behaviour, in order to improve the marketing strategies."[1]

Definitions

Neuromarketing is the study of the brain's responses to advertising, the brands encountered in our daily lives, and all the associated messages and images that are strewn throughout the cultural landscape of everyday life.
— Jim Meskauskas, editor of imedia connection

The neuromarketing is the combined use of medical technologies, with the special attention by the image of functional magnetic resonance imaging,

---

1. "Brief History of Neuromarketing", *Boricean Veronica*, November 15, 2009.

and knowledge of psychology. It is applied not to the patient, but the consumers/customers in order to hear their reactions and attitudes towards brands, products, services and even people, and thus develop promotional campaigns and institutional promotion of more effectiveness.

– McLure et al, in the journal *Neuron*

...marketing executives are hoping to use neuroscience to design better selling techniques. [...] FMRI is being exploited by savvy consulting companies intent on finding 'the buy button in the brain', and is on the verge of creating advertising campaigns that we will be unable to resist.

– Editorial of *Nature Neuroscience* (2004, p. 683)

Marketing and environmental stimuli enter the consumer's consciousness [and/or subconsciousness]. A set of psychological processes combine with certain consumer characteristics to result in decision processes and purchase decisions.
The marketer's task is to understand what happens in the customer's consciousness... [and/or unconsciousness] between the arrival of the outside marketing stimuli and the ultimate purchase decision.

– Kotler and Keller (2006, p.184)

Neuromarketing is a new field of marketing that studies consumers' sensorimotor, cognitive, and affective responses to marketing stimuli. It is based on neuro scientific consumer research and the assumption that the majority of consumer behaviour is decided subconsciously.

As Lewis puts it, "Neuromarketing is the study of how humans choose, and choice is inescapably a biological process."

Development of Nueromarketing from Sciences

Neuromarketing originates in neurosciences, and its objective is to understand the functioning of human behaviour using other interdisciplinary subjects.

Neuroanatomy – characterises the anatomical structure (morphology, connectivity) of the nervous system.

Neurology – the branch that deals with the clinical consequences of the pathology of the nervous system, as well as their treatment.

Neuropsychology – is interested in the clinical consequences of the nervous system pathology, the cognitive aspect, intelligence and emotions.

Neuroendocrinology – studies the connections between the nervous and hormonal systems.

Cognitive neurosciences – study the connections between the nervous and cognitive systems. The cognitive reorganises the different mental processes, beginning with an analysis of the perception of the environment to motion orders (through memorisation, reason, emotions and language). This defintion goes beyond the human or animal frame, and it also encompasses the processes that take place inside artificial systems such as computers. The scientific domain that studies the various aspects of the cognitive comes under the term *cognitive sciences*.

Neuroeconomy / neurofinances are interested in the decision-making processes of the economic agents and particularly in the study of their roles and, respectively, the emotions and the knowledge inside them. These branches are connected to economy and behavioural finances.

Tools Used in Neuromarketing Studies

- Functional Magnetic Resonance Imaging (FMRI) – to measure changes in the brain activity. It uses the paramagnetic properties of haemoglobin to study the various emotional changes. By seeing the changes in oxygenated and deoxygenated blood cells, the differences in the arousal of various emotions are measured.
- Electroencephalography (EEG) – to measure physiological changes like heart rate, respiratory rate, galvanic skin response and pupil dilation, etc.
- Magnetoencephalography (MEG) — to produce wonderfully detailed

3-D images which highlight activity in different areas of the brain as a person performs a task. It is used to measure the magnetic field produced by the electrical activity of the brain.

Marketing analysts will use neuromarketing to better measure a consumer's preference, as the verbal response to the question, "Do you like this product?" may not always be the true answer due to cognitive bias. This knowledge will help marketers create products and services designed more effectively, with marketing campaigns focussed more on the brain's response.

- Neuromarketing will tell the marketer what the consumer reacts to, whether it is the colour of the packaging, the sound a box makes when shaken, or the idea that they will have something their co-consumers do not.

There are two ways of eliciting information from the mind. These are:

- Priming.
- Assimilation.

Priming is the creation of an electrochemical reaction in the neural frameworks that codes for a particular word that is heard or seen. For example, if one comes across the word 'lion', this word is converted into certain codes and stored in the brain. Subsequent exposure to the word or picture or animal lion will elicit that stored code in the brain and help the person to remember lion by decoding those stored codes. The related stimuli is processed faster because of the electrochemical priming. The concept of priming is simple, although it's also a bit startling: by presenting an individual with subtle cues, one can affect the subsequent behaviour of that individual, entirely without conscious awareness of either the priming or behavioural changes.

Assimilation is the subsequent process by which new information is assimilated or incorporated into one's existing neural structures.

Advertising agencies know how important it is to repeat their messages so that priming and assimilation can take place. Priming usually occurs without the conscious awareness of the individual, even though the subsequent behaviour of the individual may be altered by the priming.

Coke vs. Pepsi

In a study from the group of Read Montague, the director of the Human Neuroimaging Lab and the Center for Theoretical Neuroscience at Baylor College of Medicine, scanned the brain of 67 people in the name of "Pepsi Challenge" after a successful campaign of a blind test conducted in the 1970s. The same test was repeated but with a difference, applying neuroscience by watching their neural activity with a functional MRI machine, which tracks blood flow to different regions of the brain. They provided Pepsi and Coke without the brand names, so that the consumers were unaware of the brand they were consuming, a blind taste test. Half the subjects chose Pepsi, and Pepsi tended to produce a stronger response than Coke in the brain's ventromedial prefrontal cortex, a region thought to process feelings of reward. The prefrontal cortex was lit up brightly. But when the individuals were asked about their preference, they responded positive for Coke as they have a pre-conceived idea and image for Coke. Their brain activity had also changed. The lateral prefrontal cortex, an area of the brain that scientists say governs high-level cognitive powers, and the hippocampus, an area related to memory, were now being used, indicating that the consumers were thinking about Coke and relating it to memories and other impressions.

Questions:

1. Most of the marketers do not know the proper applications of neuromarketing findings. Suggest a better way.
2. Does the buy button really exist?
3. Why does Coke sell over Pepsi?

Advantages

- Verbal opinion may have a conscious or unconscious bias which can be overcome through neuromarketing.

- Marketing can be done in a focussed way by directing the stimuli to the required response.
- Neuromarketing studies how a person's brain responds to advertising messages. It's the application of neuroscience to marketing.
- A real knowledge of consumer perceptions can be obtained.
- Marketers are able to measure a subject's response to specific products.
- Against the heavy cost, probing into the buy button will fetch millions.

Disadvantages
- Solely relying on the response of an unconscious decision and leaving aside the conscious mind may not give the correct answer.
- Each consumer has different stimuli and even by creating a standard pattern it is difficult to know such a heterogeneous group.
- It's also difficult to find consumers who agree to be part of a neuromarketing scientific study.
- Current neuromarketing techniques can't yet replace conventional market research in brand and advertising applications.
- The results yielded by brain studies are too general.
- The procedures involved are often too cumbersome and expensive to apply broadly.
- Knowledge addiction should be avoided.
- It is unethical to motivate or compel people by instigation to buy a product. It amounts to inculcating greed among the society.
- The buyer cannot justify more than the term "making money"
- The benefits are questionable whereas the risks are certain.
- Product craving is mentally stimulated like food craving by showing the product in an appetising way.

Technological Limitations
- 7% of patients/test subjects worldwide are not suitable for brain scans.
- Noise and density of apparatus might scare some test subjects from taking part in experiments.

- The results may be falsified due to apprehensiveness.
- The apparatus is large and inflexible and it cannot be used in the field.
- The tests require medical supervision by trained neurologists.
- Due to time and money constraints, only a small number of test subjects can be scanned.
- Strong magnets can harm human subjects if they have metal in their bodies (e.g. cardiac pacemaker, aneurism clips, intrauterine devices, some dental work, body piercings) or are carrying metal such as coins or jewelry. Such harm is not likely but the possibility does exist. Research subjects occasionally report dizziness or nausea when their heads are moved within the bore of the magnet.

General Limitations

- Accurate measurements of brain activities are limited.
- Experts with the combination of marketing and science are very rare.
- Certain emotions cannot be clearly differentiated.
- Analysis of collected data remains an enigma.
- Consumers may not like the idea.
- It may end up as complete exploitation on the part of marketers.
- It is not a fair idea to play or test with the brain.
- Consumer behaviour cannot be recreated in a laboratory.
- Time and costs prevent the testing of a large number of individuals.
- Brain activities cannot be measured against the will of the test subjects.

ZMET

Zaltman Metaphor Elicitation Technique (ZMET) is one another research tool developed by Dr. Gerald Zaltman at the Harvard Business School. It is believed that our mind conceives information in the imagery form rather than in words. Hence, the power of an image is more pronounced than the power of words. He gave disposable cameras to villagers of Nepal and asked them to take photographs of their village and then explain the photographs. He found that the photographs and their explanations were unrealistic and irrelevant. He found that in most of the pictures, legs were not shown. It is a belief that legs without slippers are considered unrespectable. Unconsciously, people avoid taking photographs of legs. This can be applicable for products also. People may not purchase the product due to pricing, unattractive outlook, etc.... but in reality, there may be some stigma attached to it. Marketers have to find out that unknown stigma to break their sales record.

The Brain

The brain has three main parts: the cerebrum, cerebellum, and brain stem. The brain is divided into regions that control specific functions.

Fig 2

Regions of the Brain

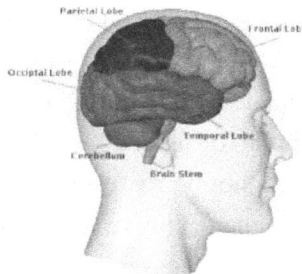

Source: picture taken and information adapted from Centre for Neuro Skills (CNS) website: www.neuroskills.com)

Brodmann Area

Korbinian Brodmann located a certain area in the brain that is more responsible for imagery and verbal recognition than the other parts of the brain. According to the *Medical Dictionary, the* Brodmann area is "specific occipital and preoccipital areas of the human cerebral cortex, distinguished by differences in the arrangement of their six cellular layers, and identified by number. They are considered to be the seat of specific functions of the brain." Hence, studying in detail about the Brodmann area will help marketers solve their problem.

THE CEREBRUM
Frontal Lobe
- Behaviour.
- Abstract thought processes.
- Problem solving.
- Attention.
- Creative thought.
- Some emotion.
- Intellect.
- Reflection.
- Judgment.
- Initiative.
- Inhibition.
- Coordination of movements.
- Generalised and mass movements.
- Some eye movements.
- Sense of smell.
- Muscle movements.
- Skilled movements.
- Some motor skills.
- Physical reaction.
- Libido (sexual urges).

Occipital Lobe
- Vision.
- Reading.

Parietal Lobe
- Sense of touch (tactile senstation).
- Appreciation of form through touch (stereognosis).
- Response to internal stimuli (proprioception).
- Sensory combination and comprehension.
- Some language and reading functions.
- Some visual functions.

Temporal Lobe
- Auditory memories.
- Some hearing.
- Visual memories.
- Some vision pathways.
- Other memory.
- Music.
- Fear.
- Some language.
- Some speech.
- Some behaviour and emotions.
- Sense of identity.

Right Hemisphere (the representational hemisphere)
- The right hemisphere controls the left side of the body.
- Temporal and spatial relationships.
- Analysing nonverbal information.
- Communicating emotion.

Left Hemisphere (the categorical hemisphere)
- The left hemisphere controls the right side of the body.
- Produce and understand language.

Corpus Callosum

- Communication between the left and right side of the brain.

The Cerebellum
- Balance.
- Posture.
- Cardiac, respiratory, and vasomotor centres.

The Brain Stem
- Motor and sensory pathway to the body and face.
- Vital centres: cardiac, respiratory, vasomotor.

Hypothalamus
- Moods and motivation.
- Sexual maturation.
- Temperature regulation.
- Hormonal body processes.

Optic Chiasm
- Vision and the optic nerve.

Pituitary Gland
- Hormonal body processes.
- Physical maturation.
- Growth (height and form).
- Sexual maturation.
- Sexual functioning.

Spinal Cord
- Conduit and source of sensation and movement.

According to the discoveries made through neuromarketing techniques, it has been found that the various factors that motivate consumers to buy certain products are:

- Self-esteem.
- Emotions.
- Consumption experience.
- Goal-directed behaviour.
- External influences.

Various findings of neuromarketing research linking science and marketing.

- *Overconsumption and compulsive shopping can be traced back to a dysfunction of the orbitofrontal cortex (ORF).*

  — Leake (2006)
- *Impulsive buying decisions are based on the emotional state of the buyer (governed by the limbic system), rational buying decisions are processed in the frontal cortex.*

  — Mucha (2005)
- *Memory retention is processed in the amygdale and ventro-medial lobes (VFML).*

  — Ambler, Ionnides and Rose (2000)
- *Irrational buying and selling is associated with the autonomic nervous system.*

  — Peterson (2005)
- "People who are more likely to purchase a product show significantly higher memory encoding than those who are less likely," explains Richard Silberstein, a neuroscientist with the Brain Sciences Institute at the Swinburne University of Technology in Melbourne, Australia.[2]
- Martin Lindstrom found that smell in particular is potent in bypassing conscious thought and creating associations with memories and emotions. Moreover, he notes that only 3% of Fortune 1000 companies have given thought to using smell in their marketing or branding, despite the claim that 75% of our emotions are generated by smell.[3]

2. Melanie Wells, "In Search of the Buy Button", *Forbes*, September 1, 2003.
3. "Sensory Branding", *Neuro Marketing Magazine*, July 7, 2007.

Area of Usage in Advertising Promotions

Posters/billboards
- location
- duration

TV/ radio adverts
- channels/stations
- time slots

Sponsoring
- celebrities
- events

Web adverts
- duration
- contents

Freebies/ promotion extras
- location
- product choice

Product development
- flavour
- smell
- colour
- health/fashion trends
- identifiying new target groups

Product packaging/design
- logo
- colour scheme

- packaging materials
- packaging size
- limited editions
- smell
- texture
- package type
- convenience

Distribution
- shelving
- product grouping
- special offers
- smell
- music
- general atmosphere /ambience
- availability
- transport facility

Neuromarketing Research
- It appears to be less transforming the existing fundamentals of the marketing discipline, as it is rather a neuroscientific consumer research technique with the potential to add significantly to the marketers' current understanding of consumer behaviour.
- It introduces the subconscious perspective with the potential to reform and extend quantitative research. Hence, it makes qualitative research more feasible than before.
- It might be the first technique which allows the inclusion of the environment into quantitative research.
- A response error of test subject is non-existent.

Ethical issues in neuromarketing:

Consumer rights rest upon the assumption that consumer dignity should be respected, and that producers have a duty to treat consumers as ends in themselves, and not only as means to the end of the producer. Thus, consumer rights are inalienable entitlements to fair treatment when entering into exchanges with other parties.

— Crane and Matten (2004, p. 268)

e.g.: consumer's right to privacy, fair pricing and free thought and choice

...do...advertising techniques...involve a violation of human autonomy and a manipulation and control of consumer behaviour, or do they simply provide an efficient and cost-effective means of giving the consumer information on the basis of which he or she makes a free choice. Is advertisement information, or creation of desire?

— Arrington (1982)

- Human beings do not have a so-called free will, as the brain reacts to stimuli split seconds before the human being recognises them consciously.
- It is an escape from ethical responsibility in general.

— Traindl (2005)

- Harvard's Zaltman, "There are people who think we can insert ideas into people's thinking."[4]

Practical experiments

Neuroco of Weybridge, England, was the pioneer company to use neuromarketing techniques by using nascent science. Later, Lewis conducted similar experiments for global players, including Bridgestone,

---

4. Wells, op. cit.

Hewlett-Packard, and some others in the food, beverage, and cosmetics industries.

Microsoft is now mining EEG data to understand users' interactions with computers, including their feelings of "surprise, satisfaction and frustration."

Frito-Lays has been studying female brains to learn how to better appeal to women. Findings showed that the company should avoid pitches related to "guilt" and guilt-free and play up "healthy" associations.

Google made some waves when it partnered with MediaVest on a "biometrics" study to measure the effectiveness of YouTube overlays versus pre-rolls. Result: overlays were much more effective with subjects.

Daimler employed FMRI research to inform a campaign featuring car headlights to suggest human faces which tied to the reward centre of the brain. In a study of men's reactions to cars, Daimler-Chrysler took three types of cars, namely, small cars, family cars and sports cars. The study showed that small and family cars are liked by men. But at a deeper level, the study found out that sportier models activate the brain's reward centres. The area in the brain called fusiform gyrus which is known to recognise human faces and shapes, lit up for the sports car. This is the same area that lights up in response to alcohol and drugs.

The Weather Channel used EEG, eye-tracking and skin response techniques to measure viewer reactions to three different promotional pitches for a popular series.

Kellogg and Proctor & Gamble are more interested in probing emotions to use for effective marketing than other companies in their field of competition. The cereal maker, with the help of hired cognitive psychologist Angela Fratianne Weltman, explored women's conflicting feelings about food. Result: women are bipolar in their emotions. They like craving food but need taste and fat. Hence, their emotions range between Special K, a low-fat breakfast food and doughnuts and great-looking legs. P&G has looked into the question of whether consumers harbour secret feelings. Nokia, a Finland based mobile manufacturer, has lately introduced a phone that expresses the moods of the user. It has a new light messaging system, an LED (light emitting diode) through which text messages can evoke certain moods by colour interpretation. It has a range of colours for choice.

Movie Trailers and Political Speeches

MindSign Neuromarketing, a company based in San Diego, California, is the first company to begin using FMRI technology to analyse a subject's brain while watching movie trailers. They have also begun to scan the political speeches of President Barack Obama. The companies which use neuromarketing very effectively are P&G, General Motor Company, Virgin and Coca–Cola.

CHAPTER 7

Unethical Marketing

Divorced from ethics, leadership is reduced to management and politics to mere technique.

— James MacGregor Burns

Ambush or Parasitic Marketing

We are all parasites; we humans, the greatest.

— Martin H. Fischer

The *Macmillan English Dictionary* defines ambush marketing as *"a marketing strategy in which a competing brand connects itself with a major sporting event without paying sponsorship fees"*.

According to Shunu Sen, *"Ambush marketing is a means of getting the maximum bang for the buck while stealing some of a rival's thunder."*[1]

The term ambush marketing was coined by the marketing Guru Jerry Welsh[2]. This type of marketing is considered unethical as it is free advertising that is not publicity but rather the act of getting cheap publicity.

1. "Ambushes a War Tactic", *Financial Daily*, September 5, 2002.
2. "Ambush Marketing to the Fore Again", *The Times of India*, September 14, 2004.

Another term is parasite living. A parasitic life means a dependent life. Ambush marketing is a marketing campaign that takes place around an event but does not involve payment of a sponsorship fee to the event. It is marketing done at the cost of another company. For most events of any significance, one brand will pay to become the exclusive and official sponsor of the event in a particular category or categories, and this exclusivity creates a problem for one or more other brands. Those other brands then find ways to promote themselves in connection with the same event, without paying the sponsorship fee and without breaking any laws. This is unethical.

Ambush or parasitic marketing is marketing which takes advantage of the publicity of a major event, specifically a sports event, without paying the requisite fee or being the official sponsor. It has affected World Cup football, World Cup cricket and the Olympics in a big way. Other events have been also affected. Laws against it have been enacted by some countries, specifically Australia, but India still needs to do a lot for the elimination of such activities. Many of the marketing legal frameworks have not been framed till date.

As in biology, parasite means those living organisms that live on food made by other living creatures, and parasitic marketing denotes taking advantage of the value of publicity of a major event which is sponsored by another company. Marketing Guru Jerry Welsh, the first recipient of the Lifetime Achievement Award for Cause Related Marketing, coined the term ambush marketing for competitive assaults on ill-conceived and poorly implemented sponsorships. He defines it as a situation in which a company or product seeks to ride on the publicity value of a major event without having to finance the event through sponsorship. Ambush marketing means companies trying to pass themselves off as official sponsors when they are not. Most of the advertising is done during major sporting events. Companies begin to advertise nationwide. It can be explained in another way thus: pretending to be the sponsor of a major sporting events without actually being one i.e. without paying the requisite fees. It comprises framing a strategy to advertise in populated places. It is being opportunistic in certain situations.

Strategic ambush[3] – ambushes that are planned, leveraged, managed, and measured exactly like best practice sponsorship, minus the sponsorship. It's not about deception or damaging the competition, and nor are IP or proximity rules breached to do it.

Ambush or parasitic marketing can be classified in two categories.

1. **Direct ambush marketing**: In the 1994 football World Cup, MasterCard received exclusive rights for using the World Cup logo, but a rival Sprints communication used the logo without permission. This is a direct attack but can be challenged by laws.

2. **Indirect ambush marketing**: Several ways of indirect ambush marketing can take place like sponsoring the broadcast of the event, sponsoring sub-categories of the major event, etc.

Kodak vs. Fuji: An example of ambush marketing.

Eastman Kodak of Rochester, NY, reportedly spend about $40 million to be the sole imaging sponsor of the 1996 Olympic Games. Fuji, another film company, which advertised on the radio and in newspapers, believed that the promotion may take advantage of the country's strong interest in sports. Fuji also planned to offer a poster series and desk calendar featuring athletes such as Dan O'Brien and Michael Johnson, both strong contenders for the Olympic team. The concern here is that people get the impression that another film company besides Kodak is an Olympic sponsor. Fuji was the sponsor for the track and field since 1990. The line between savvy marketing and deliberate ambushing can become blurred. Perhaps the best known example of ambush marketing in India came during the 1996 cricket World Cup. Coke paid Rs 40 crore to be called an official sponsor, but Pepsi's brilliant counter ad, "Nothing official about it" clearly occupied more of the consumer's mind.

---

3. Kim Skildum, "Ambush Marketing Set to Rise. Blog: Power Sponsorship," *Reid*, September 21, 2009.

Outcomes of Ambush Marketing

The main consequences of ambush marketing are:

- The commercial value of the event decreases.
- Spectators may not appreciate the environment.
- It creates an unhealthy competitive environment.
- It may adversely affect the funding of the event.
- Every company would like to be an ambusher instead of paying a huge amount for sponsoring.

Protection Against Ambushers

Australia has enacted a new law called Sydney 2000 Act to deal specifically with ambush marketing. The objectives of the Act are:

- To protect and to further the position of Australia as a participant in the Games, and support the world Olympic and Para–Olympic movement.
- To do the above to the extent that it is within the power of the Parliament to assist in protecting the relations and ensure the performance of the obligations of the Sydney 2000 Games bodies to the International Olympics Council.

In India, there is almost no protection against indirect ambush marketing. However, for direct ambush marketing, there are several laws like the Unfair Trade Practices Act, Trade Marks Act, Copyright Act, Counterfeit Goods Act and Merchandise Marks Act, etc.

In December 2006, a staff member of On Hold advertising company, placed a life-size placard of cricket legend Shane Warne wearing a branded T-shirt and the company's tell-tale 'giant hand' outside the West Australian Cricket Ground at the 3rd Ashes Test. This act of ambush marketing was noticed and the staff member was fined for 'displaying a sign without a permit', sparking a nationwide debate over wearing clothing with brand names.

Ambush Marketing on Internet

Sneaky link insertions: Some people carefully monitor the upcoming stories with the most votes on digg.com or other popular social news sites and insert comments with links to their website. When the story hits the front page or gradually accumulates visibility, the well placed links can each easily net upwards of 1,000+ visitors.

Piggyback: on an existing occurrence. To do this effectively, one should constantly push news/events related to one's target market and specific keyword-relevant searches on major online communities to a central location, like an RSS reader or dashboard.

Taking advantage of fashion/ fad: One can take advantage of the buzz around the iPhone 3G, a website about fitness, to create a stand-alone page about iPhone tips/hacks and push it out to not only the popular blogs but every single hobbyist/small-time blogger who has ever expressed interest in it.

Wherever there is cyber traffic, one can present a relevant message.

It occurs at two levels:

- onsite;
- on media.

Onsite ambush marketing happens on the premises of the event or the area surrounding it, including the approach roads and so on, using items like T-shirts, coffee mugs, roadside posters and billboards, etc. During the 1996 Olympic Games, Samsung launched a very successful onsite ambush effort in Atlanta City. Samsung, an unofficial Olympics sponsor, launched an aggressive ambush marketing scheme directed at Panasonic by taking squatters rights to a parking lot on the outer limits of the Centennial Olympic Park. Panasonic, the official Olympics sponsor, displayed its logo on the CNN tower looming over the Olympics Park. The result, Panasonic captured only 3% awareness compared to the 9% stolen by Samsung.

Why do Big Companies go for Ambush Marketing?

In spite of a good brand image and company fame, even the big multinationals go for ambush marketing, the most important reason being maximisation of returns. They want to profit through a particular event which they consider as a cash cow.

Usually, sponsorship of such an event is allocated to one big sponsor and other companies have no place in it.

This kind of ambush marketing is often done by the competitor brand of the sponsor. They believe that the sponsor will sweep up the market, so they try to steal the show.

Media ambush marketing occurs especially when a particular ambush advertisement is telecast. Say, a cricket match is being telecast and it covers a certain non-sponsor advertisement also. For example, L'Oreal hair colour ads appeared during the Lakme India Fashion Week telecasts.

It needs to be added here that in spite of the protection provided, the loopholes and opportunities will remain for rivals to undermine the mileage gained from such events. One such example is the Pepsi World Cup baseline: "Nothing official about it".

The success of any sponsorship finally rests on the sponsor's ability to sign a watertight contract, fully leverage the opportunity and always stay a step ahead of competition.

Mobile operator Hutch, one of the official sponsors of the cricket World Cup, has complained to the International Cricket Council about Sachin Tendulkar endorsing Reliance Communications' telecom products, saying it amounts to ambush marketing.

Anti-Ambush Strategies

As ambush marketing is gaining a stronger hold day by day, event organisers and sponsors are finding a way to beat the tactic through anti-ambushing efforts.

For the 2010 FIFA World Cup, South Africa, the strategies have been framed effectively by FIFA. A few are given below:

- Buying up the advertising spaces surrounding the stadium and selling these to sponsors.
- Entering into contracts with the media to provide advertisement space to the official sponsors.
- Publishing in the media and public information packs to raise awareness of the rights of the event organiser and the stringent actions that will be taken if those rights are infringed.

Fig 1

Source: Posted by Rajan Varma at his blog.

Fig 2

Source: Posted by Rajan Varma at his blog.

Undercover Marketing / Roach Baiting

This is unethical conduct at its highest and we will pursue all avenues.

— Robert Shapiro

According to dictionary.com, undercover marketing comprises advertisements using actors in real life settings to make them appear to be average people; also, people hired by a company to surreptitiously promote a product in public establishments.

The failure to disclose the relationship between the marketer and the consumer would be deceptive unless the relationship were otherwise clear from the context.

Undercover marketing is a subset of guerilla marketing where the consumers do not realise that they're being marketed to. It main aim is to create a buzz. This is not a conventional buzz where the intention of the seller is open — here the intention of the seller is hidden, disguised and misleading. It is called "undercover marketing" — marketing by masquerade, or stealth marketing. In undercover marketing, the buzz is artificially created and spread through forums, chat rooms, etc. As chat rooms and forums provide autonomy and semi-anonymity, where people perceive everyone as a peer, in the same plane as Internet chatters, the risk of being caught is less. The person / marketer as well as the marketing intention are hidden. Moreover, the costs of spending for undercover marketing are nominal whereas the results are phenomenal.

Undercover marketing is the extension of a technique called "**product placement**" used in movies (e.g. James Bond driving the newest BMW). However, while "product placement" puts products in the movies, "undercover marketing" places them in real life situations – in malls, at conferences, at parties, etc.

Sony's Undercover and Unethical Advertisement

When Sony Ericsson wanted to promote its hot new gadget, a cell phone that takes pictures, they launched an undercover campaign called "fake tourists." Sixty actors took to the streets of 10 cities. They were irresistibly innocent looking, and they were seeking a small favour from the target audience: whether they could take a picture in their cell phones. By doing so, these actors provided people an opportunity to use the mobile. The undercover operation was the brainchild of John Maron, Sony Ericcson's marketing director. Sony Corporation's latest advertising fiasco was unethical. Sony advertised its PSPs (Play Station Portables to you videogame neophytes) in many U.S cities like New York, Philadelphia, San Francisco, Los Angeles, and so on, with a concept of "urban nomads,". It painted the walls, fences and sides of buildings. This created a doubly illegal means of communication, combining the casual property damage of graffiti.

Confusion Marketing

I feel very comfortable with the way I look, and I feel very comfortable with the kind of confusion that it creates in people's minds.

– Brian Molko

Confusion marketing is creating chaos in the minds of consumers to get benefit out of that confused state. It is defined as:

A strategic marketing approach which involves making it difficult for consumers to make direct comparisons between a firm's and competitive offerings, thereby giving the firm a means of maintaining higher prices and profit margins than would otherwise be possible under conditions of easy comparisons of offerings.

– Advance dictionary of marketing by Putting Theory to Use.

It entails deliberately confusing the customers by creating a similar package or similar brand name, or similar form of advertisement of a very popular brand. Consumers go for such products, either confusing them for the famous brand or brand image. And the confusion does not end with the advertising and packaging. Placement of goods on store shelves is also a major issue, with Proctor and Gamble's Sunny Delight drink cited as an example of why consumer groups are concerned. According to recent Consumers' Association research, as many as 50% of consumers have purchased the "wrong" brand because of similarities in packaging. And the confusion does not end with advertising and packaging — because it is positioned in chiller cabinets alongside healthy fruit juices, Sunny Delight is often perceived as having health drink qualities that it does not in fact have.

Marketers deliberately want to confuse the customer by giving unrelated advertisements as these stay in the mind. The customer starts thinking about, and questioning the ad linkage with the product, and the advertisement retention and recall ability is comparatively more than other advertisements. It is also termed as hypnotic advertising as it remains in the minds of people. Sometimes, marketers deliberately confuse the customers by loading a number of offers with the product that are utterly useless and of no value to the consumer. The package looks attractive to the buyer if its benefits are not clearly studied and those conditions trap the buyers.

There are three fundamental consequences of customer confusion:
- Product satisfaction.
- Information satisfaction.
- Overall satisfaction.

Many customers end up choosing the wrong product due to confusion over the brand name, package and advertisements. This may reduce product satisfaction as the intention is to purchase a different product. Customers often feel cheated when they realise the difference.

Information confusion will lead to information dissatisfaction but not to product dissatisfaction. But a higher level of confusion leads to abandonment of the product. Communication should be clear. Every organisation should work towards increasing the level of understanding of the customer by increasing the clarity of information.

Overall satisfaction is a multi-dimensional attribute though product satisfaction and information satisfaction play a prior role.

Confusion Over Internet

Multiple products are available on the market and there is multifold information on the net. Every media educates the consumer whereas the Internet is a knowledge base to the whole society. It surpasses libraries and other knowledge providers. Libraries have to evolve online to suit people's needs. Hence, with too much information spread on the net, and the traffic it creates, there is an explosion in opinions. This has created a plethora of product choice and opinion leaders. Everything ends in a chaos of opinion. Every brand teaches a new scientific Unique Selling Proposition (USP). Customers are confused. Strategic advertising wars such as those between Blackberry and Apple, Horlicks and Complan, Rin and Tide leave customers in total confusion. The claim of every newspaper and every television channel of being number one leaves nothing but confusion. Nobody knows which is correct and ethical. In a multi-choice world, globalisation adds to the confusion. Is it possible to use a global village strategy for the local village person? A local village person may be clearly on either of two sides — falling over a global product or patriotic over a domestic product. Whereas the common man of metro cities tends to rationalise with multi-choice and often ends up in confusion.

Creating Confusion

There are various ways of creating confusion such as:

Confusion by brand name:

- Having a brand name similar to a popular brand name.
- Having a brand name that is difficult to pronounce and recall.

Confusion by the message.

- Creating confusion by advertising a product without revealing the brand name. e.g. Surf Excel. At the time of the introduction, the TV advertisement does not display the product name. It leads to confusion about, and eagerness to know, the name for about a week before finally revealing the product's name.

- Messy messages which do not explain the product's benefits or the method of its usage.

Confusion by rebranding.

- While customers are used to certain benefits of a product, the same product when promoted as providing a different benefit, may not be easily accepted. eg. Burnol, a product which was used for burn injuries rebranded itself as a solution for all types of external injuries, but is still sold for burn injuries alone.

Confusion created intentionally.

- Confusion is intentionally created to reap benefits.

Confusion created unintentionally.

- Customers may not understand the communicated message.

Multi-level Marketing

*It's different from Amway because you don't have to buy the inventory, but it is **multi-level marketing**. But that can be a valuable tool. I think any product or service that's aimed at making the fan an artist's best salesperson is very important.*

– Mike McGuire

Multi-level marketing (MLM), (also called **network marketing**) is a term that describes a marketing structure used by some companies as part of their overall marketing strategy. Network marketing is a very simple model wherein the customer finds a product he likes, becomes a "distributor" and tells people about it. Mostly, the buyer becomes the seller and so he is likely to believe in the benefits of what he sells. The products and company are usually marketed directly to consumers and potential business partners by means of relationship referrals and word of mouth marketing.

Different Models of MLM

Pyramid Model / Pharaoh Model
A successful pyramid scheme combines a fake yet seemingly credible business with a simple-to-understand yet sophisticated-sounding money-making formula. The essential idea is that the mark, Mr. X, makes only one payment. To start earning, Mr. X has to recruit others like him who will also make one payment each. Mr. X gets paid out of receipts from those new recruits. They then go on to recruit others. As each new recruit makes a payment, Mr. X gets a cut. He, is thus, promised exponential benefits as the "business" expands.

Advantages
- Easy to understand the system.
- Unfolding profit.
- Both cash value and non-cash value benefit.
- Disadvantages
- Comfortable work time.

Benefits Dwindle Steeply
- Very few top level recruits of the pyramid make more money.
- Some recruits suffer as they are unable to bring in referrals and new people into the stream of the pyramid.

8 Ball Model
The "8-ball" model contains a total of 15 members. Note that unlike in the picture, the triangular set-up in the cue game of *eight-ball* corresponds to an arithmetic progression $1 + 2 + 3 + 4 + 5 = 15$. The pyramid

scheme in the picture in contrast is a geometric progression $1 + 2 + 4 + 8 = 15$.

Matrix Schemes

Matrix schemes use the same fraudulent non-sustainable system as a pyramid; here, the participants pay to join a waiting list for a desirable product which only a fraction of them ever receive. Since matrix schemes follow the same laws of geometric progression as pyramids, they are subsequently doomed to collapse. Such schemes operate as a queue, where the person at the head of the queue receives an item such as a television, games console, digital camcorder, etc. when a certain number of new people join the end of the queue

The problem here is one of common sense. At a mere three levels deep, this would be 1,000 people. At six levels deep, it would be 1,000,000 people believing they can make money by selling. But by selling to whom?

Issues Related to MLM

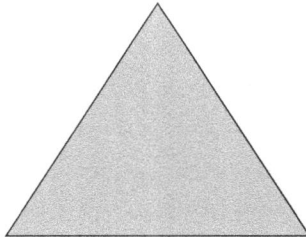

- It rejects the concept of target audience and market segmentation.
- It does not bother about need-based selling.
- The concept of dwindling money is fraudulent activity.
- The buyers and sellers are the same. So they are unable to see the negative aspects of the product.
- The profit most of them shell out is less than the money they have invested in it.

- The price of the product is exorbitant.
- If the product has quality, it can enter the competition through normal selling.
- The concept is loosely knitted as there is no strict supervision: "Be your own boss".
- Each person sells in his own profit limit due to loose supervision.
- It is based on creating rumours.
- Is the pyramid a creative idea or organised crime?
- MLM exploits the relationship of people.
- People go in blindly for MLM profits.

Nowadays, MLMs attempt to address this particular problem by limiting the number of people to four. But the same geometric expansion problems persist; the failure mechanism has just been slowed down a bit. There is now the added problem of even more unnecessary layers in the organisation.

The claim that an MLM is merely a "common man's" implementation of a normal real-world distribution channel is even more absurd in the real marketing world. Imagine buying a product or service in the real world and having to pay overrides and royalties to five or ten unneeded and uninvolved "distributor" layers. It is not only an irrational activity but also a fraudulent one. Moreover, it tries to exclude competition which is not possible in today's world. It is also termed as "multi-level mischief" as it churns through human relationships.

Black Hat Marketing

What is the difference between unethical and ethical advertising? Unethical advertising uses falsehoods to deceive the public; ethical advertising uses truth to deceive the public.

– Vilhjalmur Stefansson

This is any form of unethical marketing, and more precisely, it is applied for any form of unethical marketing on the Internet.

A **black hat** is a typical Western attire that portrays the villain or bad guy in contrast to the hero's white hat. Black hat hackers, also called black hat crackers, are the people who break the security on computers and hack information through unauthorised penetration. There are many kinds of hackers, according to their intention:

- Hackers seeking fun.
- Hackers seeking profit and information theft or information modification.
- Hackers with political motivations.
- Hackers having notorious intentions like spreading a computer virus, etc.

Various Black Hat Marketing Techniques on Internet

tAd blocking - the blocking of web advertisements, typically the image in graphical web advertisements.

Buzz word- a trendy word or phrase that is used more to impress than explain.

Cookie - information stored on a user's computer by a website, so preferences are remembered on future requests.

e-mail spam - unwanted, unsolicited e-mail.

FFA - free-for-all links list, where there are no qualifications for adding a link.

Incentivised traffic - visitors who have received some form of compensation for visiting a site.

Mouse trapping - the use of browser tricks in an effort to keep a visitor captive at a site, often by disabling the "back" button or generated repeated pop-up windows.

Keyword stuffing and irrelevant keywords – all the key words are jammed and subsequently unrelated key words are also included so that every word search will lead to that particular site.

Opt-out - (1) type of programme that assumes inclusion unless stated otherwise; (2) to remove oneself from an opt-out programme.

Page jacking - theft of a page from the original site and publication of a copy (or near-copy) at another site.

Spam- inappropriate commercial message of extremely low value.

Search engine spam - excessive manipulation to influence search engine rankings, often for pages which contain little or no relevant content.

Trick banner - a banner ad that attempts to trick people into clicking, often by imitating an operating system message

Spamming of the submission process – submission of nearly the same content in all pages.

Automatically generated doorway pages - a doorway page is created for sending a visitor to the related page by identifying the pages listed on the search engine. Doorway pages are otherwise called by many names such as portal pages, bridge pages, gateway pages, entry pages, etc. Some doorway pages redirect visitors without their knowledge by using page cloaking, which is also called page hi-jacking.

Data blogs with no unique content (also known as splogs or scraper sites) many RSS (Really Simple Syndication) feeds are just replicas of the imported data from other sites.

Code swapping – when a particular page becomes popular, it changes itself into a different page. That is, a free page, when it becomes popular, is converted to a paid one by filtering entries as the "buy me now" tag.

Astroturfing – it is one of the guerilla marketing practices. It involves creating an artificial buzz about a product or company. Postings are created in online forums, singing the praises of a certain product or service – but they aren't made by the public. They're made by shills, or people associated with the company who are paid to express a positive opinion. Astroturfing is rampant in online forums and blogs (actually "flogs," or fake blogs).

Offline Black Hat Marketing

Flyposting

Fig 3: Flyposted posters in Manchester

Souce: File:Flypost.jpg

Flyposting is the act of placing advertising posters or flyers in illegal places. In the U.S., these posters are known as bandit signs, snipe signs, or street spam, and the process of flyposting is called wheat pasting. It can stay for a longer period at the appropriate site. But it can be easily under attack. It is one of the cheapest modes of advertising whose impact cannot be underestimated.

Fig 4: Wheatpaste by Iranian street artist, Alone, in Tehran, Iran.

Source: A1onemay2007Tehran.jpg

Such advertising is seen more in the developing and underdeveloped countries. In India and other countries, it is used for political advertisements.

Fig 5

Source: File:Obama progress street art.jpg

Graffiti (singular: *graffito*; the plural is used as a mass noun) is the name for images or lettering scratched, scrawled, painted or marked in any manner on buildings. Graffiti is the oldest form of advertising. It has a historical background in the ancient Greece and Roman Empires. It is sometimes regarded as a form of art and other times as unclean and unwanted social damage. It is also considered as an art crime and sometimes regarded as a way of life and expression.

Like any art work, graffiti has many styles to offer in both pictorial and writing methods: single colour tag graffiti, multi-colour (usually two or three colours) throw-ups, stencils, stickers, wild style, a complicated and highly stylish work and block buster, which is grand and occupies more space.

In font styles, there are many like Kailgraph, Paint Cans, Magik Marker, Rap Script, Bomr, Fun Boy, Dafunk, New Digital, etc

It can be beautiful art work and can be brought under the legal system by regularising it and permitting it with the provision of certain poster / graffiti spaces like billboards.

Fig 6

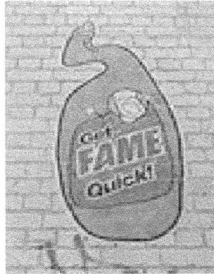

Source: Poster Art Fitzroy 1.jpg)

Street Mural Advertising.

As graffiti is the oldest possible advertising medium, it cannot be completely avoided. It may be ethical or unethical but it exists till date. But street mural advertising is the combination of street art and branding. It is done by street artists who comprise graffiti artists, muralists, wheat pasters and street installation artists. It is considered ethical also.

Glossary

A

Ad Tracking : A way to track the results of your advertising campaigns so you know which ones are bringing in revenue and which aren't. This will help you to determine where to spend your advertising budget for the best results. This is typically a software programme installed on your websites.

Affiliate Marketing: In electronic commerce, means of achieving greater market penetration through websites that target specific groups of Internet users.

Ambient Marketing: An overall feeling or mood projected by a store through its aesthetic appeal to the human senses. A brightly coloured children's room is more appealing than an area sectioned off within the adult's room.

Ambush Marketing: Creating cheap publicity by stealing the show or even without officially paying for it.

Anti-marketing: Behaviours or attitudes reflecting the view that a person or organisation rejects advocating or using any of an array of practices or principles perceived to be part of the marketing.

Astroturfing : Creating an artificial buzz about a product. This buzz is created not by the customers but by the company people themselves.

B

Back Links: Incoming or inbound links to the website or web page.

Black Hat Marketing: All unethical marketing practices are called black hat marketing. It is most relevantly used in Internet marketing.

Blog: WEB LOG. A diary or journal on an Internet site. The focus may range from the blogger's life to any subject which he is interested in. Blogs require regular updating to continue to hold the interest of visitors. The explosive growth in blogging has seen a consequent interest from companies in promoting their products and services to people that maintain or visit blogs.

Blogger: One who blogs. A person who owns and updates a blog.

Billboards: These are large outdoor advertising structures that are placed in traffic areas or common public utility areas.

Button Ads: A small version of a banner advertisement that looks like an icon which links to the advertisement landing page.

Buzz Marketing: Marketing through spreading information by creating a buzz or talk about the product around the market.

C

Cause Related Marketing: The combined effort of profit and non-profit organisations to work for a social cause. This increases the brand image of the company.

Confusion Marketing: Creating confusion among the consumers and marketing the product in the chaotic state.

Cookie: A small piece of information that is loaded on the web browser when the particular website or web page is visited.

Customer Relationship Management (CRM): CRM is the strategic process of selecting the customer that a firm can most profitably serve, and optimising the current relationship to serve in the future.

D

Database Marketing: The process of collecting the data on existing and prospective customers and using it more effectively to identify groups of customers who are similar to them.

Dot com bubble: The "dot-com bubble" (or sometimes the "I.T. bubble") was a speculative bubble covering roughly 1998–2000 (with a climax on March 10, 2000, with the NASDAQ peaking at 5132.52) during which stock markets in industrialised nations saw their equity value rise rapidly from growth in the more recent Internet sector and related fields.

Drip Marketing: A method of creating customers by repeated contacts, by providing information repeatedly and following them up till they become customers.

E

Ethical Marketing: (also called responsible marketing or sociomarketing)

Marketing concerned with conformance to morally acceptable standards of marketing.

Experiential Marketing: (also called customer experience marketing or experience marketing)

Marketing aimed at getting customers to sense, feel, think, act, and relate strongly to a brand or a company.

F

Flea Market: A place where cheap and second-hand items are sold.

Fly Posting: A type of advertisement where a poster is pasted illegally on walls and other places. Also called bandit signs, snipe signs, street spam or wheat pasting.

G

Grafitti

Green Marketing: It refers to the process of selling products and/or services based on their environmental benefits.

Green Washing: Green washing is the practice of making an unsubstantiated or misleading claim about the environmental benefits of a product, service, technology or company practice.

Grey Hat Hacker: It refers to a skilled hacker who sometimes acts illegally, sometimes with goodwill, and sometimes not.

Guerilla Marketing: An innovative way of marketing a product without much cost.

I

Inbound Marketing: Customers will contact the marketers seeking information on the product, company or the related marketing information.

Infomediary: One who acts as an intermediary while passing on information in an integrated Marketing Communications System. The term is a composite of *information* and *intermediary*. In the Internet, many websites act as infomediaries in getting a database which was not available before.

Integrated Marketing Communications: Marketing emphasising the full integration or merging of multiple, different marketing communication approaches with the aim of achieving synergistic effects and superior results relative to approaches where multiple marketing communication activities are pursued but not coordinated.

Interruption Marketing: Seth Godin coined the term interruption marketing to describe tactics that work only if they interrupt you to get your attention.

K

Keyword: A word you might use to search for a website. For example, searching the web for the keyword "Dictionary" or "Terms" might help you find this site.

Kiosk: Small area set off by walls for special use. It can be used synonymously with cubicle, booth and stall.

L

Loyalty Marketing: Loyalty marketing is an approach to marketing, based on strategic management, in which a company focusses on growing and retaining existing customers through incentives.

M

Marketing Mix

(also called the Four Ps or the Seven Ps)

The set of controllable marketing elements that marketers are able to blend either tactically or in support of broader marketing strategies — price, product, promotion, and place (or distribution)—a classification suggested by McCarthy (1960). Later extended as the 7 Ps of marketing: four Ps plus people, process, and physical evidence.

Microblogging: A multimedia blog, through which written text or any updates like photos and music are shared through blogs.

Multi-level Marketing: Creating a down line of distributors and a hierarchy of multiple levels of compensation in the form of a pyramid.

Mural: Any piece of art work, painting on wall or ceiling or any other permanent fixture or surface.

N

Network Marketing: Also called matrix marketing or multi-level marketing.

Neuromarketing: The word "neuromarketing" was coined by Ale Smidts in 2002. Neuromarketing is a new field of marketing which uses medical technologies such as Functional Magnetic Resonance Imaging (FMRI) to study the brain's responses to marketing stimuli.

O

Online Marketing: Marketing through Internet technology. It is also called Internet marketing, i-marketing, e-marketing and digital marketing. Internet marketing strategy includes all aspects of online advertising products, services, and websites, including market research, e-mail marketing, and direct sales.

Opt-in e-mail: E-mail that is explicitly requested by the recipient.

Outbound Marketing: The company will take the initiative to contact customers through telephone, e-mail, sales letter or any other media to provide marketing services.

P

Parasitic Marketing: See ambush marketing.

Permission Marketing: Marketers will ask for permission before they send advertisements to prospective customers.

Pop-up Ads: An ad displayed in a new browser window. Both pop-up and pop-under ads have been losing popularity ever since they were hijacked by spam sites. There is a plethora of toolbars and utilities available to block pop-up/under ads now, which have made them less useful. Google Adwords will not allow any pages with pop-up or pop-under adverts to be advertised.

Prosumers: The enlightened customers who are not lured by advertisements but have a clear identification of their needs.

R

Really Simple Syndication (RSS): An RSS document which is called a "feed", "web feed", or "channel" that includes full or summarised text, plus metadata such as publishing dates and authorship which can be updated.

Referral Marketing: See multi-level marketing.

Relationship Marketing: Promotional and selling activities aimed at developing and managing trusting and long-term relationships with a larger number of customers. Customer profile, buying patterns, and history of contacts are maintained in a sales database, and a service representative (also called account executive) is assigned to one or more major customers to fulfill their needs and maintain the relationship.

Roach Baiting: See undercover marketing.

S

Search Engine Optimisation (SEO): A method of improving the quality of search and optimising the traffic to various websites. There are both paid and unpaid forms of search engines.

Social Marketing: Application of commercial marketing concepts, knowledge, and techniques to non-commercial ends (such as campaigns against smoking and drunken driving) for society's welfare.

Social Networks: A social network is a social structure made of individuals (or organisations) called "nodes," which are tied (connected) by one or more specific types of interdependency, such as friendship, kinship, financial exchange, dislike, sexual relationships, or relationships of beliefs, knowledge or prestige.

Societal Marketing: Societal Marketing is basically a marketing concept that is of the view that a company must make good marketing decisions after considering the consumer wants, the requirements of the company and, most of all, the long-term interests of the society. It is derived from Corporate Social Responsibility (CSR)

Spam: Spam is the abuse of electronic messaging systems to send unsolicited bulk messages indiscriminately. Though it is referred to Internet spam, it can be subjected to other marketing methods also

T

Transaction Marketing: Marketing in a traditional way where the marketer is less interested in creating repeated purchases or loyal customers.

U

Undercover Marketing: Undercover marketing (also known as buzz marketing, stealth marketing, or by its detractors as roach baiting) is a subset of guerrilla marketing where consumers do not realise they are being marketed to. It is considered unethical.

V

Viral Marketing: It refers to marketing techniques that use pre-existing social networks to increase brand awareness or to achieve other marketing objectives (such as product sales) through self-replicating viral processes

Visual Merchandising: (VM): It is an art of presentation, which puts the merchandise in focus. It educates the customers, creates desire and finally augments the selling process.

W

Web Banner: A web banner or banner ad is a form of advertising on the World Wide Web.

White Hat Hackers: Also known as ethical hackers, or white knights, these are computer security experts, who specialise in penetration testing, and other testing methodologies, to ensure that a company's information systems are secure.

Word of Mouth Marketing (WOM): Passing on the information of the product by talking about it. Nowadays, online WOM is also possible.

Bibliography

1. Robert Bartels, *The History of Marketing Thought*, 3rd ed, Publishing Horizons, Columbus, 1988.

2. Stanley C. Hollander, Kathleen M. Rassuli, D. G. Jones, Brian Dix, Laura Farlow (2005). "Periodization in Marketing History", *Journal of Macromarketing*.

3. Jay Carnold Levinson, *The Guerilla Marketing Handbook,* Houghton Mifflin, 1984.

4. David Shani & Sujana Chalasani, "Exploiting Niches Using Relationship Marketing", *Journal of Consumer Marketing*.

5. Sumantha Dutta, *Relationship Marketing – A Paradigm of 21st Century*, Kolkatta.

6. S. M. Jha, *Social Marketing*, Himalaya Publication, New Delhi.

7. Fritz Wolfgang, *Internet Marketing & Electronic Commerce*, 3rd ed, Gabler Verlag, Wiesbaden.

8. Deckmyn, "When Customers Want Email, not Spam", *Computer World*, vol 33, 1999.

9. William F. Arens, *Contemporary Advertising,* McGraw Hill Company.

10. Dr. N. K. Sehgal, Gronroos, 1994, 2007.

11. Christopher Payne, *Relationship Marketing Creating Shareholder Value*, Ballantyne.

12. M. W. Vilcox, *Contemporary Issues in Business Ethics*, Nova Science Publishers, Hauppauge, NY, 2007, 1-3. (ISBN 1-60021-773-7).

13. David B. Wolfe, Robert E. Snyder, *Ageless Marketing: Strategies For Reaching The Hearts And Minds Of The New Customer Majority*, Dearborn Trade, p. 359.

14. Alan Mitchel, Harper Collins Business, 340 pages.

15. Seth Godin, *Permission Marketing*, Simon & Schuster, 1999.

16. Seth Godin, *All Marketers are Liars*, Penguin Publications, 2009.

17. John Hagel III John and Marc Singer, *Net Worth*, Harvard Business School Press, ISBN -0-87584-889-3, 1999.

18. Melanie Wells, "In Search of the Buy Button", *Forbes*, September 1, 2003.

19. "Sensory Branding", *Neuro Marketing Magazine*, July 7, 2007.

20. "Ambushes: A War Tactic", *Financial Daily*, September 5, 2002.

21. "Ambush Marketing to the Fore Again", *The Times of India*, September 14, 2004.

23. Kim Skildum, *Ambush Marketing Set to Rise*, Blog: Power Sponsorship Reid, September 21, 2009.

24. Justin Kirby & Paul Marsden, *Connected Marketing*, Elsevier, 2007.

25. Mark Butje, *Product Marketing for Technology Companies*, Elsevier,

26. Larry Bailin, *Mommy, Where do Customers Come From?* 2nd ed, Morgan James Publishing, 2009.

Index

www.ingramcontent.com/pod-product-compliance
Lightning Source LLC
Chambersburg PA
CBHW021712210326
41599CB00013B/1630